GW00481350

You Are
What
You Think

© Ocean Books 1998
All rights reserved.

You Are What You Think

A guide to the
technique of self-suggestion.

Tycho Photiou

There are many quotations included within this book. They are the words of wise men and women through the centuries, up to, and including, the present day. Many of the quotations are from various religious texts, particularly Buddhism and Christianity.

Some of the relatively modern sources are acknowledged in the bibliography. Whilst the publisher has made every effort to obtain permission for the quotations wherever appropriate, this may not have been possible in every case. We would therefore like to thank everyone who contributed to provide the wonderful and rich teachings that you will find within these pages, and accept our apologies if any modern sources have not been adequately acknowledged.

Where there is no attribution given to the quotations, they are the authors own.

Ocean Books
228 Baker Street,
Enfield EN1 3JY
Middlesex.
Tel (0181) 350 9600

1st Edition - Published 1998

Printed in Great Britain by
St Edmundsbury Press Ltd, Bury St Edmunds, Suffolk.

AUTHORS NOTE:

The English Language has a slight weakness in that there is no word as yet to represent "he or she" in written language - the author would like to rectify this problem by making the following definitions:

> They = he or she
> Their = his or her
> Them = him or her.

These definitions aren't really original, they are already used in this way considerably in spoken language, so, the author now feels that it is about time to extend their use to the written form.

ACKNOWLEDGEMENTS:

I would like to thank my sister, Andrea, for proof-reading the initial manuscript of this book and for all the kind help, inspiration and support that she has given me throughout my life.

I would also like to thank the numerous friends who gave me so much encouraging feedback, especially Suzette Ansah for her helpful advice in proof-reading the final manuscript.

Contents

Preface

Andrea Photiou

Take a bed of soil that is exhausted and unnourished and try to grow a fruit tree. The tree may survive but it will be weak and vulnerable and the fruit will be sparse and unpalatable. However, had the soil been cultivated and nourished beforehand the tree would have had a much better chance of growing well, with strong roots and luscious fruit, just as nature intended it to.

Somewhere through time we human beings seem to have lost the ability to naturally enrich ourselves. This is partly due to the path of our western civilisation and society, and partly because life itself can be exhausting and disillusioning. Many of us seem to have lost the ability to love who we are and celebrate our existence. When problems present themselves in life, we can often become lost in a fragmented maze of stress and disillusionment.

You are what you think is the first of a series of books that aims to help us return to our true nature, opening the doors to our full potential, and in so doing discover a richer and more exciting way to live. This book is a tribute to the potential of every individual. It tells us how to begin the process of cultivating our minds and setting up the conditions in which we can best grow and develop.

You will find a step by step guide to ways of controlling the negative effects of life, and at the same time be given methods to develop and reach a better quality of life by simply adjusting your own attitude and belief systems.

Within each of us is an ocean of untapped potential, outside of ourselves is a world that belongs to us by the grace of simply being born into it - and more than this, we are surrounded by other people who are ready to become our teachers, our friends, even our lovers, and share the journey with us.

Almost nothing is impossible if you believe in your dreams and the power that you have within you to make them come true. But, you must believe in your own capabilities and have faith in life. Through a renewed understanding of your own needs, resources and potential, you will have taken the first step on a most exciting journey.

Introduction

This book will introduce you to the immense power that you have within you to influence *every* aspect of your life. How much you get out of it depends on how you read it. If you read it as you might read a novel, you will, hopefully, find it interesting but it probably won't change your life. However, if you participate and take the advice suggested, do the exercises, and carry out the self-suggestions recommended you will be amazed at how rapidly and dramatically your life will change.

However many holy words you read, however many you speak;
What good will they do you if you do not act upon them?
                          THE DHAMMAPADA

There are now many books on the market written on "The power of the mind" but is it really the mind that has the power? The first question that I want to consider is: "Where is the source of this power?" Is it really the thoughts and the imagination which are faculties of the mind that are all powerful, or is the mind just a tool which enables us to tap into a deeper power within us? Is it possible that the source of the power is in the subconscious, or maybe from our soul or essence, or from an energy flowing through us and through all of nature, or even from universal consciousness?

Whilst it is worth giving some thought to all of these possibilities, the answer is obviously not a straight forward one because we are complex beings and one aspect of us affects every other. I believe that the "power" isn't actually from the mind, this is just a powerful tool that enables us to programme suggestions into our subconscious. The subconscious itself is also a tool that enables us to tap into an enormous source of energy that we are usually unaware that we have access to. The mind and the subconscious are incredibly powerful tools that we permanently have at our disposal to help us achieve great heights.

In this book you will learn how to make suggestions to counteract all the negativity that you may have been hearing throughout your life, by reprogramming the subconscious for health, wealth, happiness, or whatever dreams you desire. You will learn how **you create your reality by every thought and every image that goes through your mind**. Your thoughts can affect the biochemical processes going on in every cell of your body. Everything that you think about has some effect - this is particularly true with regards to your health and general well-being. **The contents of the subconscious affect every aspect of your life.**

In this book you will learn how to relax and then transmit to your subconscious specific, positive, realistic suggestions. You will also discover a means of harnessing the energy within you to achieve goals which you previously thought impossible. By appropriately adjusting your mind, reprogramming your subconscious and channelling the energy within you in a positive way you could improve your health, become more relaxed, learn more easily, improve your memory, become more successful in many ways, and cure a whole range of illnesses from the common cold to cancer.

You Are What You Think

You Are What You Think

A man becomes what he thinks
about all day long.
RALPH WALDO EMERSON.

Emerson was undoubtedly not the first to realise that our thoughts influence every aspect of our lives. Our thoughts determine our emotions, our circumstances, and most importantly - the attitude we take towards our circumstances.

The greater part of our happiness
or misery depends on our dispositions
and not on our circumstances.
MARTHA WASHINGTON.

Our thoughts can work for us, to enhance our lives, or, if our mind is filled with fear, negativity and dread, it can make our lives much more difficult than it need be. For example, depending on our self-image and our attitude towards whatever we are doing, we can feel really tired all the time or feel full of energy, we can either feel afraid to talk or act in a given situation or feel totally confident, we can feel sick or we can feel healthy, we can feel miserable about the way things are or we can accept life with a smile. **Our whole reality depends on the way we think.** Negative thoughts and emotions affect not only our mental and emotional state but they also adversely affect our health. **The mind is responsible not only for our happiness and success in life but also for our health and fitness.**

The benefits that we receive when we are able to be in charge of our mind and only permit the presence of thoughts which enhance our well-being and make us feel more in harmony with life are enormous. The way we think is habitual and *it is* possible to change, and as our thoughts change, our lives change, since our life is a direct result of every thought that passes through our mind.

Every good thought you think is contributing its share
to the ultimate result of your life.
GRENVILLE KLEISER.

Every thought we think, and every word we speak has both internal and external consequences. If we want to be healthy we must dwell on health, not on pain, illness and disease - we must think health and talk health - in this way, good health will inevitably follow. The same is true of wealth. If someone desires material wealth, there is much more chance of this manifesting in their life if they can develop a *prosperity consciousness* rather than focus on debts, bills and poverty.

You can think your way to failure and misery,
but you can also think your way to success and happiness.
NORMAN VINCENT PEALE.

The quality of our relationships are determined by the quality of our thoughts. This is obvious really, since the way people relate to us is determined by what we give out, and what we give out, is, in turn, determined by our thoughts.

If we think kind, loving thoughts,
we will have kind, loving relationships.

The reason that thoughts are powerful has both a very simple explanation and a more complicated explanation. The complicated explanation involves the idea that all material reality

- the whole universe - is a product of consciousness, and so all of our thoughts, beliefs and ideas have some effect on "external" reality. If this idea is correct it would mean that their is, in fact, no such thing as objective reality, since reality cannot exist independently of the consciousness which observes it. The simple explanation is that our thoughts are the initiators of every word we speak and every action that we take, and it is our words and our actions that determine our lives.

THE POWER OF WORDS

A man who speaks bad words,
will attract bad circumstances into his life;
A man who speaks loving words,
will attract good circumstances into his life.

Sometimes we may not even need to say the words out loud since our thoughts can be reflected in all of our non-verbal behaviour. If we are listening to someone with judgement, this attitude will radiate out in our facial expressions and our non-verbal behaviour and so have its effect on people around us. Conversely, if we listen to someone with openness and love, we will automatically transmit this feeling, and so bring about different effects on those around us. Usually, the strongest effect that we have on people with whom we interact, is through our words, relationships can be healed by simply changing the way we talk to someone or about someone.

Here are a few quotations from Buddhism and Christianity, that express the power of words in various ways:

Refrain from false or malicious speech.
THE BUDDHA.

*Kind words are like honey - sweet to the taste
and good for your health.*
PROVERBS 16, 24.

*You will have to live with the
consequences of everything you say.
What you say can preserve life or destroy it;
so you must accept the consequences of your words.*
PROVERBS 18, 20

If, while engaged in conversation, someone compliments us and tells us something like: "You are looking really well today, I have never seen you looking so radiantly healthy", this will generally never fail to have at least some effect to make us feel good.

*The music that can deepest reach,
and cure all ill is cordial speech.*
EMERSON.

Many people engage in speech not for the value of the message that they have to convey, but simply because they like the sound of their own voice. So it is a very useful question to ask yourself sometimes: **"When you convey an idea to someone, is the emphasis more on how you can make your point, or on how the listener can benefit?**

*If a man's words are no better than silence,
then he should remain silent.*
BUDDHIST PROVERB.

This is a very wise saying that applies to many social situations not only ones of conflict. It conveys an excellent message to those people who speak, not because they have something to say, but because they just love the sound of their own voice.

It is very important to be aware that the statements you mutter to yourself at various times during the day, can have an enormous effect on how you feel. A few examples of expressions to avoid are:

1) *This job is a pain in the neck!* - Unless you are painting the ceiling, this expression is better avoided. If you do say this often and the suggestion penetrates into the subconscious it is possible to end up with a stiff neck just from doing the washing-up, even if your neck muscles are healthy!

2) *I am sick and tired of doing this!* - What effect do you think this expression would have on the subconscious? It is not very likely that saying this will actually make you vomit, but it can't have a very positive effect on your physical or emotional well-being. It is fairly certain that expressions like this, used often, can result in a greater level of tiredness than is normal for the job that you are doing. You may say that complaining makes you feel better, but although you may feel a brief sense of emotional relief, it certainly isn't good for you in any true sense, on the contrary, when the subconscious receives the negativity it does far more harm than good.

3) *I am fed-up of doing this!* - If this is registered by the subconscious then, due to the power of our words, the state of feeling "fed-up" will occur, but more because of what you are thinking than what you are doing.

4) *These calculations give me a headache!* I believe that there isn't a calculation on earth that could give me a headache, because I love calculations. If you end up with

a headache after doing some mathematical or financial calculations, then the cause of the problem is the suggestion that calculations can create a headache and not the calculations themselves.

5) *It's a miserable day!* - This is a very common expression in England because the English love to talk about the weather, but the fact is that *the weather can't be miserable,* only people can be miserable about the weather. As soon as you say "it's a miserable day" you are making it so for yourself and those in your company. There is very rarely any justification for getting depressed about the weather - just look at the rain and smile and think about how much life on earth depends on it. If you can actually have nice associations for the weather it helps when you wake in the morning since the weather has quite an influence on what we feel when we get up and look out of the window. Making friends with the weather can make an enormous difference to your life.

Regarding the last of these, once the body is made comfortable by providing it with suitable clothing for the day, the mind is then free to enjoy all the varied weather conditions that nature provides us with. For instance, a heavy downpour can give a nice feeling of seclusion under an umbrella surrounded by a curtain of rain and is also quite invigorating. A dull day is cosy and private, and there's a quietness that is fairly relaxing and even soothing. Bursting sunshine is enlivening and energetic. Frosty mornings are magical and frost with sunshine is very, very beautiful. A morning fog is a shroud of mystery. Snow is fresh and so atmospheric that one cannot help smiling at passers by. A breezy autumn morning can be quite playful and a red sunrise is positively glorious. It is a small step to adapt to the morning weather, rather than fighting against it and moaning that it is the cause of our bad mood.

I have wandered slightly from the main point of this section, but the intention is to emphasise that the words we speak and the thoughts we think are extremely powerful, and every aspect of our lives can improve if we are able to adjust our thoughts and the attitude we take towards every challenge that we face.

THE MIND AND THE IMAGINATION

It is not enough to have a good mind.
The main thing is to know how to use it.
RENÉ DESCARTES.

One of the most dominant faculties of the mind is the imagination. **The contents of our imagination affects every aspect of our lives.** Negative images held in our mind can cause adverse internal effects which dissipate our energy. Conversely, positive images create good effects which boost our energy. If we could, in every moment, use our imagination to create positive images of ourselves and the world, this would have the effect of boosting our energy, improve our relationships and help us feel happier about life. There is probably not one adult human being on this planet who has not at some point felt happy, sad, angry, frightened or excited due to the contents of their imagination.

The imagination is an incredible thing, we can use it to create within our mind almost anything we want. At any moment we could imagine that we're doing any number of things, such as standing on the moon, lying on a beach in the Caribbean, talking to the queen, flying through the air, riding in a speed boat, eating our favourite food, taking a space walk, getting attacked in the dark, caught in a fire, involved in a plane crash. The possibilities are endless. In fact, there is almost nothing that we cannot experience in our imagination.

Something that many people don't realise is that each person's imagination works in a different way. Some imagine visually and can "see" an image when they close their eyes, while others just get a vague impression of what something looks like but can't actually "see" it. Some can imagine audio sounds as if they are hearing them while others just get an impression of the sound without internally hearing anything. The same is true of touch, smell and taste. If one hundred people were asked to close their eyes and imagine sitting on a beach, the clarity and sensory content of the image would vary enormously between people. For some people everything is so vivid that it is almost as if they are experiencing the imagined event in the moment while for others it is a very vague impression. Despite these enormous differences between people, everyone has this amazing tool called the imagination, and everyone can use it to go anywhere or do anything they want, even though the clarity of the image may vary from one person to another.

So, if at any point in this book I make a statement such as "imagine an apple", don't worry if you can't internally see it, as long as you can at least form some vague image of it, then that will do.

If someone feels sad, fearful or worried because *there is* something in the environment to generate that condition, then this is a normal, beneficial reaction. For example, if someone is running towards us wielding a knife, it is totally normal and natural to feel fear. However, there is another type of fear that is totally destructive, and that is the fear created by simply holding horrible images in our mind. If we *just imagine* someone running towards us wielding a knife, the fear reaction performs no constructive purpose whatsoever. Sometimes the imagination can create a fear as strong as that created by a real event, and the physiological consequences can be just as fatal as if the danger were real. There is a sad story of a man on whom a cruel joke was played - his head was placed on a block and he was told that he was to be beheaded. When his fear was at its height and his attackers finally had him convinced that the cold steel was about to sever his head from his body they finally dropped a single drop of ice cold water on to the back of his neck and he died of heart failure from the shock - such is the power of the imagination.

IMAGINATION "CHANNELS"

I like to think of the imagination as a series of programmes that we are watching, sometimes we decide what to watch and other times the programmes just appear and we watch like an obedient slave. Sometimes we may be watching our favourite channel: "The tranquillity channel" or "The wonderful life channel", but at other times the mind might be stuck on "The disaster channel", "The hard life channel" or "The horror imagination channel." If a negative thought or image comes to our mind, we may dwell on it and give it all our attention in a similar way to the automatic response that occurs if an exciting but violent scene appears on television. Very few people actually enjoy watching scenes of horror and violence, but given the opportunity most people can't resist it. To resist putting our attention on something which is both powerful and negative requires a considerable awareness. With awareness we can begin to transcend the automatic response of putting attention to our worries and fears except when it may benefit us to do so. This is, however, easier said than done. If, while imagining something horrible, we just tell ourselves: "Let me think about something nice, what shall I imagine?" then we are not very likely to have much luck. What we need to do is think in advance, (in a way that I shall now describe), of a wonderful scene that we can always use whenever the occasion arises. You need to form a scene of peace and tranquillity that is very clear in your mind, then, when you start imagining something horrible you can immediately replace it with your beautiful image. You will then not just passively watch scenes of disaster happening in your imagination, but *decide* what the contents of your imagination shall be, just like changing the channel that you are watching on T.V. But this is no small challenge, it is as difficult as switching the television off just as an exciting bit comes on, and so it requires a firm resolve that this is what you want, and that you will make the effort to carry it through every time that your mind starts dwelling on any unpleasant thoughts or images.

So, try it now, sit somewhere on your own and just give yourself a little time to relax, then tell yourself: "For the next ten minutes I am only going to think pleasant thoughts and picture wonderful images". It is when you try to do a seemingly simple exercise like this - when *you decide* what your mind should think - that you may come to realise that *you* are not your mind, but simply the observer of your mind, and your mind doesn't always want to do what *you* tell it to do.

There are just as many possibilities of positive images as negative, so think about a strong positive image. Go to a wonderful place in your mind such as a beach, a cottage in the mountains, a beautiful park, or a desert island. Endeavour to make the image as clear as possible. For example, you could imagine yourself lying on the beach under a palm tree in the Caribbean, feeling the cool breeze against your skin, hearing the splashing of the waves, feeling the texture of the sand, seeing the sky, and so on. You may want to feel the sun shining down on you and the wind on your face, or hear the sounds that might accompany the experience, or feel yourself walking, running or moving within the image. Whatever scene you choose, make it one with as much sensory content as possible. You can call this your "tranquillity image", try to have it ready for whenever unpleasant images arise.

When your mind tries to give you a hard time be firm, but gentle with it, and tell it that you have no interest in dwelling on those negative images and that it is time to go to your place of tranquillity. This will work if you really want it to.

THE SUBCONSCIOUS

The subconscious is that part of us which contains all the information concerning how we function physiologically and how we feel about ourselves. Almost every aspect of our internal bodily functions and our behaviour is under subconscious control. We don't need to decide when to blink, breath or digest our food - our subconscious can deal with these processes on its own. The heart rate, chemical processes in the liver, production of urine and all other so-called involuntary processes are under subconscious control. It has been said that nature wouldn't trust man to digest his food by his own efforts because through his carelessness he would soon starve to death!

Our behaviour, and the way others see us, is determined by our subconscious programming. Aspects of behaviour that are under subconscious control include facial expressions, hand and body movements, posture, tone of voice, eye movements, and many other aspects of how we project ourselves in the world. **The subconscious is so powerful that any suggestion that penetrates into it, both good and bad, will have a profound effect on our lives.** The information contained in the subconscious influences our body by working on a part of our nervous system called the autonomic nervous system which controls many aspects of our bodily functions. It influences the workings of both our voluntary and involuntary functions such as breathing, blinking, digestion, blood temperature, heart rate, the reproductive functions and the hormonal and circulatory systems. The fact that the "involuntary" functions are, in fact, under voluntary control, provides a very good reason why we should avoid the use of this term, and, since these functions are controlled by the autonomic nervous system, the term "autonomic" functions is used in it's place.

The autonomic nervous system operates without the necessity for our conscious attention. Without our conscious awareness it happily proceeds to carry out its job of pumping the heart, digesting food, healing damaged tissue, producing sperm or ova and maintaining our blood pressure and temperature at the optimum values for our efficient functioning. It also regulates the menstrual cycle in women. The instructions for all this incredibly efficient functioning is contained in the subconscious when we are born. But, unfortunately, this programming is influenced by everything we experience from the time of our birth.

*The body maintains itself according to the
information contained in the subconscious.*

Besides these physical processes the subconscious programming determines our actions and behaviour. If our subconscious is programmed for success and happiness with a positive self-image then we will be much more likely to become successful and happy. Conversely, if it is programmed for misery and failure with a negative self-image then that is what will manifest in our lives.

As I will explain in more detail in the next chapter, **we can adjust the contents of the subconscious by what we suggest to ourselves.**

THE CENSOR

In our normal everyday life there is a kind of barrier between the mind and the subconscious - this is called a censor. The presence of this censor is essential because it acts as a filter to stop much of the information, that we are continually bombarded with, from getting through. I sometimes like to think of this censor as a guard, similar to a sentry guard protecting a building, where the guards job is to stop information getting through to the subconscious too easily. If the censor were not present then as soon as we watched a television commercial telling us to buy a product we would just rush out and get it. In our normal, everyday lives, the censor acts as a good servant filtering out information which would otherwise corrupt our perfectly efficient subconscious programming.

The problem with the censor is that if we want to make positive changes to our lives by adjusting our subconscious programming then the suggestions may have trouble getting through. If this were not the case then we could simply make a decision to be more healthy, confident and successful, state a few positive suggestions, and then whatever we desire will be realised.

Even though the censor is present, if we hear a statement or message enough times, something does get through to the subconscious and this has the effect of slightly modifying our behaviour or our physiological functions. For example, if we hear enough times that a certain product is marvellous, we will eventually want to try it. Similarly, if we are told often enough that we are a failure, then, as soon as we start to believe it, we begin to make it come true. **No matter who we are, or what opinions we have, if we hear a certain view enough times we will eventually believe it.**

If we could find a way to put the censor to sleep and get positive suggestions through to the subconscious then it could take just a few moments to programme in a life-changing suggestion - as long as there is not too much negativity to counteract. However, if we are just in a normal state of consciousness and there is a lot of negativity to deal with then it may be required to repeat the suggestion many times over several weeks or longer. For example, if we have been told ever since a very young age that sex is dirty, naughty or immoral, then it will take more than just a few simple suggestions to counteract the effects of these destructive negative beliefs. There is a way of getting suggestions to bypass the censor and get through to the subconscious more efficiently, this will be explained in the next chapter - *the technique of self-suggestion.*

LOOK AFTER YOUR MIND

When people will not weed their own minds,
they are apt to be overrun with nettles.
HORACE WALPOLE.

It is amazing how many people in our society put so much more emphasis on physical health rather than on mental or spiritual health. In preparation for the day ahead many people may spend an hour or so in the bathroom seeing to their bodies but how many would spend that much time in the morning seeing to their minds or their spirits? If someone has a physical sickness, they generally do something about it, they may exercise, stay in bed, improve their diet, take medicine, and so on. However, the same is usually not true for mental, emotional or spiritual conditions unless the sickness becomes so grave that we just can't ignore it.

A tidy mind has the power to identify and deal with problems as they arise, whereas a mind that is already overrun with problems becomes powerless to identify and deal with them. It is not very sensible to leave mild mental conditions such as worry, pessimism, boredom or depression, untreated when there is nearly always something that we could do to help alleviate these conditions. Here are a few of the various ways that you could take care of your needs for mental and spiritual hygiene:

1) Meditate every morning for a short while, between five and twenty minutes.

2) Use positive self-suggestion.

3) Listen to relaxing music in the morning while looking forward to the wonderful day ahead of you.

4) Enhance your feeling of appreciation for life by focusing on everything that you have, rather than putting your attention on what you don't have.

5) Just sit and *let yourself be* for five minutes or so without the intention of doing anything.

6) Be silent and still - focus your attention on the sensory stimulation in your immediate environment - listen to the sounds around you, observe the colours and shapes, feel the textures against your skin.....sharpen your awareness.

7) Practice releasing anger, resentment, hate and other negative emotions and replacing them with feelings of compassion, love, understanding, generosity and other positive emotions and states of being.

8) Pray.

If you spend just 15 minutes every morning and evening doing any of the above you will be amazed at how quickly you will begin to feel the positive effects.

This emotional, mental and spiritual house-cleaning service may function best to highlight that which needs to be dealt with, in other words it enables you to be more in touch with yourself. Sometimes the clearing and cleaning process will involve dealing with negative thoughts and feelings such as worry, fear, anger and resentment. If, for example, you go to sleep with a problem and wake up with the worry still hanging over you, one possible way of dealing with this would be to hold the thought "today I will seek an answer to this problem". The worry then becomes not a dwelling in crisis, but a problem solving exercise - this is a healthier way to deal with a worry than to just pretend it isn't there.

KEEP A POSITIVE ATTITUDE

*It is the way we look at
the scenery that needs changing,
and not the scenery itself.*

Attitude means the way that our mind is adjusted to look at any situation. A positive attitude enhances the value of every experience. Our attitude determines the internal effect that any experience has upon us, it's importance cannot be overestimated, it determines not only whether we are happy or sad but also whether we are healthy or ill. Our attitude to life makes life how it is: If we think life is great then it is; if we think life is terrible then it is.

*By adjusting your attitude appropriately your world
can look however you want it to look.*

Our attitude affects every aspect of our lives, it can lift our energy and make us feel elated or it can take us down into a destructive state of lethargy and depression.

If we say: "that experience had a really bad effect on me" this is not strictly true, it was *our attitude to the experience* that had the bad effect and not the experience itself. Two people could pass through identical unpleasant experiences and one could become ill while the other may learn and develop from the experience.

> *Men are disturbed not by things that happen,*
> *but by their opinion of the things that happen.*
> EPICTETUS.

Our attitude is determined not only by our thoughts and beliefs but also by our subconscious programming. When there is a stressful situation present, each person responds in a different way, some may be very slightly affected, while others become ill. The way we respond to stress is far more important than the stressful event itself. **It is not a stressful event that can make us exhausted or ill - it is the body's response to the stressful event that can do the damage.**

With a positive attitude we not only make the most of everything that happens to us in life, but we also enhance the positive effect that the experiences have on us both emotionally and physically. Even if we are in physical pain, it's what we do with that pain that determines how much we suffer. If we curse it and wish it weren't there, then we will suffer, not so much from the pain itself, but from our attitude to it.

> *Pain is inevitable.*
> *Suffering is optional.*
> M. KATHLEEN CASEY.

If we have a problem, it is very important to remember that the way we look at it is our own choice. Some problems sometimes seem insurmountable, but if this is true then the best action that we could take is to adjust our attitude to the problem - if we can adjust our attitude to a problem such that it doesn't bother us anymore then it is almost as good as if it is solved. In fact, it is true to say that many problems that we have, are created by the belief that we have a problem! **If we have a problem, what is more important is not the problem, but our attitude to it.**

In addition to adjusting our attitude to the problem we must look at the part we play in its creation and/or perpetuation.

> *Every problem is an outward manifestation of our state of consciousness. When our consciousness is clear and at peace, the problem disappears.*
> *ARNOLD PATENT.*

In social situations, our interpretations and reactions to events or to other people's comments about us is determined mainly by our attitude, which, in turn, is influenced by how we see ourselves. If we think that we are very sensitive and easily hurt, then the "cruel comments" will hurt us much more than if we see ourselves as fairly thick skinned.

> *Sticks and stones may break my bones but words can never hurt me.........*
> *unless I believe that they can.*
> *ADAPTED PROVERB.*

We are only bothered by another man's words or actions if we allow his words or actions to bother us. If we have self-respect then we are less likely to be bothered by what others say and think of us.

We are injured and hurt emotionally,
not so much by other people or what they say or don't say,
but by our own attitude and our own response.
MAXWELL MALTZ.

The way that you verbalise in your own mind is much more important than what others tell you. If someone says something offensive to you, then it is what you tell yourself after, that determines whether you get offended or not. You can get very upset thinking, "why does he say such horrible things?", or you can just realise that he is probably throwing the insults at you because of his own insecurities, feelings of inferiority, or whatever.

No one can make you feel inferior
without your consent.
ELEANOR ROOSEVELT.

It is important to be aware, however, that the person who is trying hard to make us miserable has, indeed, a problem, and is to be sympathised with - it is their own shortcomings and lack of awareness that leads them to attack. However, even if you are aware of this on an intellectual level, it is not always possible to remain unaffected by the abusive comments of another, because, although our minds have the ability to reason, we are still human and our emotions can still get bruised. It's important, in this situation, not to feel that we've failed because we didn't rise above it, since what we have actually done is to limit considerably the negative effects due to our awareness and our attitude.

LOOK AT WHAT YOU'VE GOT

*To be upset about what you don't have
is to waste what you do have.*
KEN KEYES JR.

One of the main causes of dissatisfaction in life is the fact that **we tend to see more value in what we don't have than what we do have**.

A few years ago I wrote the following poem called *look at what you've got* about the importance of keeping a positive attitude:

*I have learnt a lesson from two of my friends,
who made me realise on what happiness depends.
They both have exactly equal things in life,
a job, a car, a home and a wife.*

*Yet one is happy the other is sad,
one thinks life is good, the other thinks it's bad.
The difference is in their point of view,
and the way they look at what they do.*

*When it rains my sad friend will sulk all day long,
but my happy friend will smile and sing a happy song.*

If someone else has something that we don't have, we might say "aren't they lucky, I wish I had that", or "I wish I were in their position", however, the reason that what they have looks so appealing is simply because we don't have it, or because we are not them.

The other man's grass is always greener.
PROVERB.

A certain level of dissatisfaction is totally normal and healthy, this is human nature and it is partly what keeps us striving for new things, always wanting to improve our situation and have new experiences, but if we are perpetually dissatisfied then life begins to lose its value. We need to reach a situation where we can have enormous appreciation for what we've got, while still striving to improve our situation and develop. It is a sad situation if we spend our lives setting ourselves ambitions which once satisfied are immediately replaced by another, never appreciating what we have, who we are and the journey we are on while moving towards our goals.

As you wander through life, whatever be your goal,
keep your eyes on the donut and not on the hole.
PROVERB.

The focus upon what we don't have, rather than what we do have, applies to many situations that cover all our needs such as air, food, water, sex, and health. We can only truly appreciate water when we are thirsty. If we were dying of thirst we may think that we would be so happy when we get water, but when it comes and our thirst is satisfied we usually forget about its value. The same could be said of air or any other commodity that we have and take for granted. If we were suffocating and gasping for air our life's ambition at that moment would be just to get some air into our lungs - but as soon as we are breathing normally again the air seems to lose its value.

If we are ill, we may promise ourselves that when we get better we will appreciate our good health, but once the illness is over we usually just revert back to our "normal self" taking for granted all the wonderful things in life that good health brings. Having said that, if the illness is severe and long-lasting enough the sufferer usually develops sufficiently to then truly appreciate good health when it eventually comes. In a similar way, money can only be truly appreciated if we are poor and we don't have much of it. A poor person may say: "I would be happy if I was rich" but he probably wouldn't just as the thirsty man is no happier once he has quenched his thirst.

If we don't have a car we may think that obtaining one may make us the happiest person in the world, but as soon as we get one we realise this isn't so. What often happens with many people is that they then begin to want a better, faster and more expensive car or a sexy partner to go with it. Some, after achieving this type of goal, simply turn to other material desires, like a new kitchen, a bigger house or whatever. With regards to relationships, a person may feel in great need of a partner if they haven't got one, but once they get one the need obviously diminishes, and if the partner becomes permanent they may even wish that they were free again! Someone in this situation, may decide to separate from their partner, but as soon as they do so they will still feel a deep sense of dissatisfaction and may even wish that they were back with their partner again.

Dissatisfaction ultimately arises from within. If we have something wonderful in life that is "always there", we may not ever realise it's value until we lose it.

You don't know what you've got 'til it's gone.
PROVERB.

This is sometimes true of a loving parent or partner - we may only realise how wonderful they are during a period of absence, either temporary or permanent.

Absence makes the heart grow fonder.
PROVERB.

We need to try to reach a position where we can see the value in what we have while still striving towards better things, in other words, *learn to appreciate.*

The healthiest attitude
is an attitude of gratitude.

In fact, the word *gratitude* means to have a grateful *attitude.* Our lives would be so much richer if we could learn to appreciate everything we have - our food, our water supply, the people in our lives, our health, our friends.............everything.

Many christians say "grace" before meals to give thanks for their food. This can be a very constructive activity if it is done to show a genuine gratitude for the food that is about to be eaten and not simply as a ritual without any thought. The words are not as important as the feeling of appreciation.

If you are not a christian you can still say grace but instead of saying: *"For what we are about to receive may the Lord make us truly thankful - Amen".* You can say something like: *"I greatly appreciate the universe for providing me with this wonderful food and drink - Cheers God".*

In fact, when giving thanks in this way, it doesn't really matter a great deal what you say - it is the feelings behind the thoughts or words that are the most important.

THE OPTIMIST AND
THE PESSIMIST

The two opposite attitudes of positivity and negativity are portrayed by those of an optimist and a pessimist. An optimist is someone who looks at the bright side of every situation and expects the best to happen whereas a pessimist looks at the dark side of every situation and expects the worst to happen. An optimist says that a bottle is half full whereas the pessimist says that it is half empty. An optimist takes the view that life is generally good, with a few difficult experiences which are challenges for our growth and development, whereas a pessimist says that life is generally bad with one hard experience after another and only the occasional happy event.

An optimist may see a light where there is none,
but why must the pessimist always run to blow it out?
MICHEL DE SAINT-PIERRE.

The two opposing mental attitudes of optimism and pessimism are not innate characteristics since someone isn't born an optimist or a pessimist -they are ways of looking at life - mental habits that we have picked up. So, if you are a pessimist, you can, if you want, learn to look at life more optimistically simply by practising seeing the bright side of every situation. What most people don't realise is that the optimist usually has more luck in life than the pessimist due to the fact that we create our reality by our expectations. If we imagine that something bad may occur, we are starting to set up the conditions for it to occur. **If we can eliminate negative attitudes from our lives and look at the future with an optimistic smile then things will rapidly change** - opportunities arise, luck starts to come our way, and all kinds of unexpected things start to happen.

Look at the following conversation between an optimist and their pessimistic partner:

O: Do you fancy going to the park on Sunday?
P: Yes, I would love to go, but it will probably rain and then we will have a miserable time.

O: No, I doubt that it will rain, but even if it does we can still enjoy it, if not in a different way.

P: How can we enjoy it if it rains? We will probably both catch flu and be in bed for a week.

O: That's not true, the rain can't give you flu unless you get soaked through to the skin and you get freezing cold. The rain is wonderful - it freshens things up and it makes everything greener and smell better.

P: That gives me no pleasure, walking in the rain is certainly not my idea of fun, and anyway I always get flu if I get wet.

O: So, don't you want to go to the park on Sunday then?

P: No, I prefer to stay home, *it is safer!*

This little conversation is about a trivial issue, but it highlights a very important aspect and consequence of the pessimist's mentality: *The thought that things might go wrong stops a pessimist from experiencing life to the full.* A pessimist tends to imagine everything going wrong: "I won't go and talk to her because she might be unfriendly", "I would love to leave my job, but if I do I will probably never find another one and I will end up broke, bored and could even lose my house".

A pessimist often gives the excuse: "If I expect the worst and it doesn't happen I am pleasantly surprised but if I expect the best and it doesn't happen then I am disappointed". I don't think that this justifies the negative outlook, because to go through life expecting the worst to happen deteriorates the quality of life. In addition, holding an attitude of dreadful expectation is more likely to make any situation worse.

Many people have the attitude of not expecting too much because they can't stand the disappointment. I think that the key lies in looking forward to something with an open mind and a peaceful acceptance if it doesn't occur. In addition it is always possible to have a "plan B" which is just as nice but depends more on yourself than external factors. Here is another conversation between our two friends:

O: I can't wait for ...., I'm really looking forward to it.
P: But it may not happen and then you'll be really disappointed.
O: No, I won't.
P: How come?
O: Well if it does happen then that'll be wonderful, and if it doesn't I have an alternative plan. Either way I would have enjoyed looking forward to it.
P: I wish I could flow with life like that.
O: You can, I will teach you how if you want..........

Another excuse often made by a pessimist is: "to consider that things could go wrong is being realistic". This is not true, since the reality is that many of the worries about the future actually never happen, and the worries that do materialise probably only happen because the worry sets up the conditions that can cause them to happen.

> *When I look back on all these worries, I remember the story*
> *of the old man who said on his deathbed that*
> *he had had a lot of trouble in his life,*
> *most of which had never happened.*
> WINSTON CHURCHILL.

Just as a pessimist will see the bottle as half empty rather than half full, they will also put most of their attention on what they don't have rather than on what they do have, and on what they don't want rather on what they do want. If attention is always put on the bad then this is what we are giving our energy to and therefore this is what we are more likely to create for ourselves in our life.

What a wonderful life I've had!
I only wish I'd realised it sooner.
COLETTE.

Since problems can often be so helpful in moving us towards developing, many people choose to replace the word "problem" with the word "challenge". If we can learn to see our problems, not as burdens, but as opportunities for growth, then life will become an exciting challenge.

Where a pessimist sees a problem,
an optimist can see an opportunity.

If you now realise how your expectations determine what manifests in your life, and if you accept that what you focus your attention on, tends to manifest, then you will realise that it *always* pays to expect the best. A positive, optimistic attitude can enhance your health, happiness and success in every area of life.

Be realistic - plan for a miracle!
SHREE RAJNEESH.

NEGATIVE CONDITIONING

It is very important to consider the question: "Is pessimism learned or innate?" In other words, if someone sees life in a negative way is it just the way they are, or is it more a mental habit that they have picked up during the course of their life?

Research shows that the average child hears 14 negative

comments to every 1 positive comment all through their childhood. For example the average child, on an average day, while being looked after by an adult may be told: "Don't touch that; You naughty boy; That's dirty; Be careful; You are a very bad girl; Don't behave like that; Stop that; That is very dangerous; Don't be so silly; Oh no, look what you have done!" and so on. And every now and again they may be told: "Well done, that's very good". Most children are brought up in this way with a vast imbalance between negative correction and encouraging advice. In an ideal world it would be nice to cut out the negativity completely and only give out positive advice and comments but in the real world this isn't always possible, when interacting with children it is sometimes essential to tell them: "You shouldn't do that" or "that is not very nice of you", but if for every statement like this we gave them a positive statement to provide a balance then they would grow up in a much healthier, well-balanced way.

The types of comments that are most harmful are those that give a negative self-image, "You are a bad boy" is much more damaging than "Don't do that, it can be dangerous". The first is a statement which affects the child's self-image, whereas the second affects his view of the world. To give a child an awareness of dangers is essential but it isn't very healthy to hear "it is dangerous" too often, since fears can sometimes be instilled in a child when the intention may be to give an awareness of what *could be* dangerous. It is possible to give a child an awareness of the dangers of cars, water, heights and wasps, without instilling a fear of these things. To say "Be careful!" too often can have an unbalancing effect giving a child a false impression that *life is dangerous* rather than certain things in life *can be* dangerous.

The self-image of children is moulded by their parents and other adults in their environment, which in turn affects their behaviour, their personality *and even their health*. If children are criticised, patronised and taught by ridicule and humiliation, they will very quickly learn self-doubt, insecurity or guilt. Negativity is passed down from one generation to the next like a long-lasting contagious illness. This "illness" will only be "cured" when a certain level of awareness is reached.

If you have children, you may want to be their sole teacher so that they don't get "corrupted" by outside influences, but the truth is that life is their teacher and you are their guide. It is important to guide children so that they can get the best out of every situation and use each experience to learn and develop from.

The teacher may have the map,
but it is the student who must make the journey.

Some people feel victims of their childhood if they were bombarded with negativity and discouragement; but blaming our upbringing is not helpful, there is a much more beneficial alternative, and that is to release resentment and blame and to take responsibility for our own lives from this moment on.

Some of your beliefs originated in your childhood,
but you are not at their mercy unless
you believe that you are.
JANE ROBERTS.

Once we reach a certain level of awareness, we can do something about all the negative conditioning that we have had up to this point in our lives. We can take responsibility by using the technique of self-suggestion, to counter-balance the effects of most of the negative suggestions that we were subjected to during the formative years of our childhood.

Achieve
What
You Believe

Achieve What You Believe

No man knows what he can do until he tries.
PUBLILIUS SYRUS

To become fulfilled we need to make use of our potential. We must discover our life's mission, set ourselves goals and in moving towards our goals, live in harmony with what we feel deep in our heart is right for us. Every human being is capable of so much, but most people are unaware of their true potential. If you truly want to do something and you have faith in your abilities then there is almost no dream that is beyond your reach.

A man's reach should exceed his grasp,
or what's a heaven for?
ROBERT BROWNING.

It is generally true that **if someone has done something, then you can do it also.** You may say: "No, this is not true, we all have different abilities, some people seem to be good at everything but I have my limitations - I couldn't climb a mountain!" Well, as soon as you say this then the truth is that you couldn't climb a mountain because you believe that you couldn't.

Limited expectations yield only limited results.
SUSAN LAURSON WILLIG.

It is true that we all have different abilities, but why is this the case? Our abilities are primarily created by our self-image and our imagination, **what we can do in life is created by what we believe we can do.** So, we must look carefully at any self-limiting beliefs that we may have in order to release ourselves from the constraints that we put upon ourselves by holding to these views. **Our beliefs create not only understandings and explanations, but also limitations.**

*Our limitations are created by
what we believe our limitations are.*

There are always exceptions that can be used as arguments against this last statement, for example: A blind man shouldn't make it his aim to become a professional photographer or a painter, just as someone deaf shouldn't make it their aim to become a professional musician. Although, having said this, Beethoven wrote his magnificent ninth symphony after becoming deaf. So, maybe anything can be achieved if the will is there!

Where there's a will, there's a way.
PROVERB.

There are many well-documented examples of people performing amazing feats to save their loved ones, such as the mother who was able to lift a car to save her son trapped underneath it, when under normal circumstances she couldn't lift even a fraction of the weight of the car. She didn't have time to reason and think about the impossibility of the challenge, she just summoned up an energy which we are usually unaware that we have access to, and she did it. Imagine what we could all achieve if we were permanently connected to this source of energy. If you truly believe that you can do something and you hold onto that belief in spite of obstacles and disappointments, then you will ultimately achieve it. Conversely, if you believe that a certain goal is unrealistic, then it is extremely easy to prove yourself right, since, the chance of attaining that goal would be very remote due to the fact that you considered it impossible to start with. **What you believe is realistic, is realistic, and what you believe is unrealistic, is unrealistic.**

*Most people achieve what they achieve
because they believe they can achieve it.*

MAINTAIN A POSITIVE SELF-IMAGE

*Our self-image is the single,
most important factor in determining our
success and happiness in life.*

A negative self-image is one of the principal causes of failure. Our self-image creates the reality of who we are. The most destructive self-talk regarding self-image is to say things like: I am weak, I am bad, I am afraid, I am stupid, and so on - as soon as we say "I am ...." our subconscious immediately begins to work on making the words become reality. So try to always maintain positive self-talk - I am strong, I am good, I am courageous, I am intelligent, I am healthy, and so on.

*Every cell in your body is totally aware of how you
think and feel about yourself.*
DR. DEEPAK CHOPRA.

Try to be happy with who you are, learn to love yourself, not in an egocentric way, of course, but with a wholesome self-respect and develop a positive image of yourself as a confident, happy, good person. If you love and accept yourself as you are, this will lead to a positive change, as opposed to, if you curse and punish yourself. Simply accept where you are now, while realising that you are on a path of development which can take you to wherever you have the confidence and imagination to go.

It is important to realise that if you hate yourself or see yourself as a hopeless failure then you are less likely to develop than if you learn to love yourself. This may sound like a contradiction, and you may argue that "someone will only change if they have a characteristic that they don't like and therefore want to change". However, if the desire to change is motivated by a lack of self-esteem, this will not be conducive to positive change. Imagine, for example, an obese person who has a negative self-image and hates themself because they can't stop eating. This self-hate causes a self-perpetuating vicious circle - the lower the self-esteem the greater the refuge taken in food, which in turn lowers the self-esteem even more. Also, if their self-esteem is very low, then they may not feel worthy of the good that they think would come to them if they were to lose weight. Much of this occurs at a subconscious level; they may say that they deserve all the good luck that may come to them if they were to attain their ideal weight, but subconsciously they may not feel that they deserve it. This is one of the reasons why many people are held back from attaining their dreams and ambitions - on a subconscious level they don't feel that they deserve the "luck and good fortune" that would come into their life if they attained their goal.

What is required in a situation like this is to put attention on positive qualities and work on developing a positive self-image. A fat person will only start to overcome problems of over-indulgence, (if that is the cause of their obesity), when they start to focus on other positive aspects of their character and learn to like themselves - if they do this, then the problem, if it is caused by low self-esteem, will just disappear.

The image contained in the subconscious, acting through the autonomic nervous system, controls our posture, tone of voice, strength of voice, eye movements, facial expressions and body language - these convey to the world, without our conscious intention, how we feel about ourselves and this in turn influences the quality of every interaction. **A person with a confident self-image always sits, stands and walks with a healthier posture than someone with an inferiority complex.**

What makes for a straighter spine,
vitamin D, milk or self-esteem?
DR. DEEPAK CHOPRA.

If we can have self-acceptance and self-respect and refrain from judging, blaming or criticising ourselves, then, as self-awareness develops everything around us will improve. The image we have of ourselves is created by a combination of the verbal suggestions we tell ourselves and the visual image that we have of ourselves. **Our self-image is, by far, the most important factor in our lives.**

CREATE WHAT YOU EXPECT

All things are possible to he who believes.
JESUS CHRIST

Let us suppose that you want to make a certain change in your life. It could be anything from learning to smile whenever it rains to curing a major illness that you may have. **The magic formula for success is: *Want, Believe, Expect.*** All three are necessary in creating your reality. To be able to achieve success, it isn't quite enough just to *believe* that you can do it, you must have such confidence that you *expect* the desired outcome is going to materialise. Expectation is one step further than belief because if we *expect* good luck to come our way this leaves less room for doubt than if we *believe* that good luck will come our way. So, in considering the importance of faith and trust, maybe what Jesus should have said is:

All things are possible
to he who believes and expects.

Imagine that it is your desire to drive to a foreign continent, how far do you think you would get if you never expected to arrive? More than likely you probably wouldn't even bother to leave! In addition, if you believed that you could go but you didn't expect that you would ever get around to it, then you wouldn't!

We have much more chance of achieving what we expect than of achieving what we want. The chance of manifesting a desire is increased even more if we can expect it to such a degree that we can give thanks for it, even before it materialises.

If you want to give a public talk but you don't believe that you can, then you can't. If you want to give up smoking and believe that by using suggestion you can but you expect that you will fail, then you probably will fail. If you *want* to be full of energy and not get tired at the end of a busy day and you *believe* that by using self-suggestion you can feel much healthier at the end of the day *and you expect* that you will be successful, then you will. If you expect that you can become healthy by using the power of your mind then you can, but if you expect that you can't then you can't. **What you expect becomes your reality.**

The fact that outcomes in our lives are primarily determined by what we expect to happen, explains why so many people keep themselves in poverty - whilst they *want* to be rich, they *expect* that they will remain poor, instead of expecting wealth.

The principle of life is that life responds by corresponding;
your life becomes the thing you have decided it shall be.
RAYMOND CHARLES BARKER.

43

This is also expressed very concisely in the fairly well-known proverb:

Life is a self-fulfilling prophecy.
PROVERB

NEGATIVE EXPECTATION

Some people go through life always thinking the worst could happen, and often the very things that they dread manifest in their life. They use their mind to create the horrible reality that they expect. They say things like· "I was worried that this might happen and now it has."

The thing that I feared
has come upon me.
THE BIBLE.

We can create the negative reality that we dread by simply expecting it. This "condition" can be referred to as "dreadful expectation" and is also sometimes called "catastrophic expectation". For example, if someone worries continually that their partner may be unfaithful, or that they are going to get a serious illness, or that their relationship will break up, or that they will never get anything good out of life, then they are, through their thoughts (and hence their behaviour), setting up the conditions for these things to occur.

Although dreading that something may happen is not as strong as expecting it to happen, the effect is still powerful. The thoughts that we hold in our mind, of dire events and circumstances that might happen, are well worth trying to avoid - we shouldn't hold in our mind for long, any thought or image that we don't want to come true.

It would not be at all helpful, if, after reading this section, you become worried about worrying, since this will only create anxiety which won't help in any way. I would like to point out that there are certain worries that are very natural such as worrying that a loved one may come to some harm, or that a burglar might enter your home when you are alone. These types of thoughts are really more "concerns" rather than "worries", and I would say that having concerns of this type do not increase the chances of them coming to pass, since we do not want, believe, or expect that they will happen - we simply hope that they won't. In addition, these concerns do not usually modify our behaviour and therefore do not create the conditions that may cause them to manifest. Strictly speaking it is only our long-term behavioural patterns, brought about by our thoughts, that can have the effects of setting events into motion. This is very different to having concerns about possible dangers that might be present, which may help us to modify our surroundings, (such as fitting burglar alarms or smoke alarms), in order to minimise the risk of the dangerous situation coming to pass.

POSITIVE EXPECTATION

As well as creating problems for ourselves by dreadful expectation, the reverse, fortunately, is also true. **We can use our mind to create the wonderful reality that we desire by forming a clear image of the result that we desire and then expecting it to come true.**

> *Every day holds just as much promise*
> *as we're capable of expecting.*
> KAREN CASEY / MARTHA VANCEBURG.

Some people say: "I always expect things to work out for the best, and they usually do". So, if someone expects to be successful at an interview, find the ideal job, have good health, get exactly what they want out of life, then they are, through their thoughts and behaviour setting up the conditions for these things to occur. Of course, good fortune doesn't always happen over-night, it may take quite a while, but as soon as you picture yourself as a success, you will *immediately* start to move in that direction.

Although, the positive expectation of success is very likely to bring about the desired outcome, it is important to avoid an anxious attachment to the desire - a kind of "desperate yearning" which can often have the reverse effect and inhibit the movement towards achievement. A desperate yearning is often doomed to failure since it holds within it an inherent dread of failure, and with the emphasis on the failure this is what can happen.

So, how does "the magic formula" work? Associated with the want or desire is an *intention* and this intention provides the motivating force which brings into play the creative imagination that visualises the desired outcome as if it has already been achieved. The belief in a desired outcome provides the *attention* necessary to start the process of making the goal become realised. Keep in mind that the attention that we put on a desire or goal provides it with the energy required to make it materialise.

The expectation of success is what promotes *action* which is essential before we can achieve anything, since, however good our visualisations are, we will never achieve anything if we just sit there hoping and waiting.

> *Even if you're on the right track,*
> *you'll get run over if you just sit there.*
> WILL ROGERS.

So, the path to success is a six part process: *desire, belief, expectation,* linked to *intention, attention and action* - where the first three are the initiators of the last three.

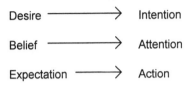

Desire $\longrightarrow$ Intention

Belief $\longrightarrow$ Attention

Expectation $\longrightarrow$ Action

If any of these items are missing then the desired outcome is less likely to be achieved.

IMAGINE IT AND CREATE IT

*Whatever the mind can conceive
and believe, it can achieve.*
NAPOLEON HILL.

You can use the enormous power of your imagination to be, to have, or to do, whatever you have the capacity to dream about. Imagine yourself now - head up, good posture, walking tall, feeling confident, a smile on your face, you are ready to conquer the world. Close your eyes now and form this image as clearly as you possibly can. Picture yourself exactly how you've always wanted to be. In your imagination you are now a successful, intelligent, kind..........person, (fill in the blank with whatever quality you wish to have). Do you notice a change occur within yourself as you form this image? If you can imagine it with any clarity then it should certainly have some effect on the way energy flows through your body. The stronger the image that you form in your mind the greater the emotional and physical effect. This doesn't need to be a fleeting thought or image that will be exchanged by some negative self image as soon as you finish reading this sentence, try to hold a positive image in your mind for the next few hours, days, weeks or indefinitely. The result of holding this positive self-image for a long time is that it will have the effect of reprogramming your subconscious to create this new reality.

> *It is through the imagination that*
> *the formless takes form.*
> CATHERINE PONDER.

Now, let's look at a few examples of the things that you could do if you really wanted to. You could walk on hot coals, lie on a bed of nails, eat fire, tolerate extreme cold, hang from your teeth, demolish a house with your bare hands, climb a high mountain, go to the south pole, walk across the Sahara desert, tolerate intense pain, lift up a car, talk confidently in front of a thousand people, obtain any qualification, tame Lions, fly across the Atlantic ocean sitting on top of an aeroplane, walk across Niagara falls on a tight rope, be shot from a cannon, and so on. Maybe you wouldn't want to do most of these things (especially the last!), but the important thing to realise is that if you so wished you are probably capable of most of them, because they have all been done by "normal" human beings.

> *Any idea seriously entertained tends to bring*
> *about the realisation of itself.*
> JOSEPH CHILTON PEARCE.

Every invention, building, piece of furniture, work of art, piece of clothing, film, book, or any man-made item that you can think of, came into existence initially as a thought in someone's mind.

> *Imagination precedes manifestation.*

It is interesting to think that four thousand five hundred years ago the great pyramids were just an image in someone's mind, and that person decided to make their vision become reality. The same is true of any man-made structure or object. This book and every idea in it (whether original or not) had to occur in my mind before it manifested as written words on the page. Every technological development originated first as an idea in someone's mind, every calculating device, computer, fax, photocopier, television, radio, telephone, camera, and so on. The same is true of every business, every piece of farmed land, every landscaped garden, in fact, almost everything that man has ever created.

> *Whatever you want to create in your life,*
> *you must first create in your imagination.*

A few impressive examples are: The great wall of China which is 3,460 km long; The Taj Mahal in India which took 20,000 workers over 20 years to complete; The 82 km long Panama Canal, which links the Pacific and Atlantic oceans; The Channel tunnel linking England and France under the sea; The vehicle assembly building at Cape Canaveral, USA, built to house the construction of the Apollo spacecraft (just the doors are as tall as 70 men!). Each of these great accomplishments originated as an idea in the mind of someone who realised their immense potential to make things happen. You too have that potential.

The important thing to realise from all this is that **if we want to create something new or do something different with our lives we have to imagine it first.**

> *Every big accomplishment in history has come about*
> *by someone holding to their vision.*

The more aware you are of your unlimited potential, the more you can achieve. Mankind only managed to reach the moon because someone, at some time, imagined it happening and believed it to be possible. There is almost no limit to what mankind can ultimately accomplish.

If you can imagine it, you can achieve it.
If you can dream it, you can become it.
WILLIAM ARTHUR WARD.

Having a goal inspires action, and all goals originate as a dream. You cannot set yourself a goal if you don't first have a dream. Dreams inspire us to move in a certain direction - you imagine a place you would like to go or a position that you would like to be in, and then you set yourself a goal to get there. Without dreams and goals we lack the motivation which drives us towards self-development.

Hold fast to dreams for if dreams die,
life is a broken-winged bird that cannot fly.
LANGSTON HUGHES.

Everyone needs to dream, not only to give our life direction, but also because fantasies are known to be very good for our emotional health. But to make a dream come true you must first set yourself a clear goal based on the dream and then go into action, setting up the conditions to make your dream become reality. The successful position that someone finds themself in today, is due to the dreams of yesterday.

What we are today comes from our thoughts of yesterday,
and our present thoughts build our life of tomorrow,
our life is the creation of our mind.
THE BUDDHA.

SET YOURSELF GOALS

The tragedy of life doesn't lie in not reaching your goal.
The tragedy lies in having no goal to reach.
BENJAMIN E MAYS.

All the goals that we set ourselves are meant to take us on the path towards greater success; but what is success? For one person it may be to gain a position of respect or prestige, for another it may be to earn lots of money, while for someone else it might be to achieve spiritual peace or enlightenment. Often our beliefs about success are conditioned by society's values which may be inconsistent with what our true individual values are. If this is the case, we may not follow our own path and release our full potential because of pursuing "what we are meant to do".

A successful person is one who is able to fulfil his potential
by listening to the wisdom of his own heart.

It is important to assess exactly what success means to you. Many people go through life dissatisfied and unhappy wishing things were different to how they are, but they don't really know what they want, in fact most people have no idea what they *really* want in life. It is a very obvious but important point that, **before we can get what we want, we need to know exactly what it is that we want.** We also need to know what type of desires are most likely to bring us closer to happiness. As well as asking ourselves what our goals are, we must ask ourselves "why are these goals important to me?"

At this point I would like to distinguish between two very different types of desires, namely, egocentric desires and spiritual desires. As the name suggests egocentric desires are the yearnings for things which can feed the ego, such as the accumulation of money and material possessions, the need to "win", the need to be told how physically attractive you are or what a wonderful person you are and the need to be popular. In contrast spiritual desires are those desires which are more transcendental such as the desire to spread love, the desire to help every living creature with whom you interact, the desire to establish peace and harmony in your life, the desire to increase your ability for unselfish giving and the desire to be loved. Regarding the last of these it is important to realise that the desire to be loved is a spiritual desire, which is very different to the desire *to be told* that you are loved which is an egocentric desire. In a similar way consider the difference between the terms "good person" and "do-gooder". The former usually refers to someone who wants to help people irrespective of what they get in return in the way of gifts, thanks, or food for the ego, whereas the latter tries to do things for people so that everyone can *see what a good person they are.*

Obviously, there is nothing wrong with wanting to be materially successful, physically attractive, or enjoying the sense of achievement when we get something that we have been working towards. What can be the problem is when we think that our happiness depends on the achievement of these desires - it is this attachment to desires that we need to transcend. It is normal to want to be appreciated when we do someone a favour, but if it is the sole motive for doing something then it can very often lead to frustration, sadness or disappointment, especially when our ego isn't satisfied by the thanks that it desires.

Many people when asked the question: "What do you really want?" may answer "lots of money", but the important question to then ask is: "Why do you want lots of money?" What is it that money will give you that will make you happier? In what way would you change your life if you were very wealthy?

Here are two questions for you to ask yourself:

1)   If time and money were no object how would I live in a way that would make me happier?

2)   What can I do in life to serve others which will make me feel happier with who I am?

We are much more likely to derive satisfaction from our achievements if they are not totally self-centred but contain some aspect of what we can do for others.

> *The purpose of human life is to serve,*
> *and to show compassion and the will to help others.*
> ALBERT SCHWEITZER.

If one has a dream it almost always has an element of wanting to become more popular with others - and this is not at all a bad thing. We are human and it is almost impossible to totally transcend egocentric desires. However, we must be aware that it is the realisation of our spiritual desires that will bring us closer to true happiness.

Now, just for a few minutes think about what success means to you. Try to form an image of yourself as a successful person, or if you already consider yourself successful, you can imagine yourself as even more successful. Think about what you would do for a living. What sort of life-style would you have? How would you feel? How would you look? In what way would you help people or the planet? Stop reading now and write down on a sheet of paper one paragraph starting with: "I would feel really successful if...........".

To be truly satisfied in life you must discover not only your personal goals, but also your true mission, which is the reason that you are here on this planet. Your mission involves not just getting what *you want* in life, but finding out what you can do to serve others, while making use of your full potential. When you discover this you will know that you have found your purpose because your life will feel extremely worthwhile. To discover your "mission" in life, listen to what your inner voice is telling you. Look carefully at your deepest life-dreams - these hold the secret to your life's mission.

At this point I would like you to stop reading, and write down a *dream-list*. This is a list of absolutely *everything* that you would love to do assuming no limitations. Avoid thoughts like "no, but I'm not clever enough to do that" or "that would take too long, I haven't got the time or the money". Your dream-list could contain anything from between twenty and one hundred goals, some of which are totally within your reach now, and others which you might not be quite ready for yet.

You could write down your dream-list in a totally random way, putting down whatever comes into your mind, or, if you prefer, you could classify it according to the following categories:

1) Spiritual goals, e.g. to spread love or attain inner serenity.
2) Emotional goals, e.g. to have more self-confidence or to be more tolerant.
3) Physical goals, e.g. to have perfect health or to go for a daily run.
4) Intellectual goals, e.g. to get a degree or to learn a new language.
5) Financial goals, e.g. to start a business or find enjoyable work.

If you are thinking about changing your profession, or maybe you want to start moving in a new career direction, then what you should think about is this: What would you like to do for a living that you would even pay to do? The ideas that come to mind hold a lot of information about the direction that you could be moving in, if you take the required steps. But remember, the first step to going anywhere, is to know where it is that you want to go.

Now, take your dream-list and rewrite it on two separate sheets of paper headed "short-term goals" and "long-term goals". Include all goals which you could achieve if you devoted enough time and energy to their attainment. (Try to keep in mind that your limitations are created by what you believe your limitations are). Next, take a clean sheet of paper and write these goals down again in order of decreasing priority - most important at the top.

As you are well aware, goals are never achieved by simply wishing and hoping, *action is the key*. So, it is now time to brain-storm again. For your first goal, write down a list of as many activities that you can think of that would be required to achieve this goal. Write down as much as you can, from the most important actions to the almost insignificant. Now, arrange your activity list or action plan in order of *increasing* priority, (simplest first). This action-plan could contain anything from making a phone call to moving house. For every action that you intend to make, imagine yourself doing it easily and successfully.

Hold an image of yourself in your mind as if you have already achieved the success you desire. The important point about all goals that we set ourselves is that they give us a path to travel. Indeed, **it is our goals that determine our direction in life.**

To be what we are, and to become what we are capable of becoming is the only end of life.
ROBERT LOUIS STEVENSON.

As you are on the path towards achieving your goals, it is extremely important to be open to the lessons that life is giving you, so that you can continually reassess whether the path that you are following is the path that you want to continue along or whether it might be appropriate to change direction.

The great thing in this world is not so much where we are, but in what direction we are moving.
OLIVER WENDELL HOLMES.

It is also very important to not be so wrapped up in the attainment of the goal that we forget to appreciate who we are and what we already have. When we allow this to happen, the inner turmoil and constant activity can destroy the inner peace and harmony that is essential to feel truly fulfilled.

Success is as much about living in peace with your own individuality, as it is about achieving your goals.
ANDREA PHOTIOU.

I explained previously the distinction between egocentric desires and spiritual desires, but throughout history "wise masters" have taught that to find happiness we have to be free of all desire, I would now like to deal briefly with this important point.

HEALTHY DESIRES VERSUS ADDICTIVE DESIRES

It is fine to have desires and to set goals, but we must avoid making the mistake of thinking that our happiness depends on the satisfaction of our desires and the achievement of our goals.

Happiness can only be felt if you don't set any condition.
ARTHUR RUBENSTEIN.

Desire is a useful driving force to help us move forward in life, however, if it is coupled with a continuous feeling of dissatisfaction, then something must be going wrong. **Desire is the motivating force that keeps us moving and developing by promoting action.** It is the intense desire that distracts us from the moment, that I referred to earlier as a desperate yearning, that we need to transcend. If we *yearn* to be rich, the yearning will stop us from being happy, and although we may think that becoming rich will make us happier, this is very unlikely, since, once we attain the focus of our desire, we will either, immediately set ourselves another goal which we will need to achieve before we can *finally be happy*, or, we will hold ourselves back from feeling happy due to the fear of losing that which we have gained.

It is clear that if we think that we are not happy, because we don't have something that we want, then we need to look within ourselves for the source of our discontentment. It is a grave error to think that winning something, owning something or even achieving something will make us happy. It is addictive desires that we need to learn to let go of. If we have an addictive desire, one of two things may happen - either it will be satisfied or it won't be. As I have just pointed out, if the desire is satisfied it won't lead us to happiness, and if it is not satisfied we will be in a constant state of tension created by the belief that that is what we need to make us happy. The result of an unsatisfied addictive desire could be anger, frustration, boredom, sadness, resentment, or any other negative emotion.

> *It is ironic that it can often be the desire that we think is meant to lead us to happiness, that keeps us unhappy.*

But not all desires create unhappiness. If we have a healthy desire to achieve something, then that desire will motivate us to move forward and if it is not satisfied - no problem. We simply flow with life and trust that whatever happens is right. So, we see that the important point is not to let go of all desires, but to learn to trust in life and feel that whatever happens is right.

BE CONFIDENT - RISK IT!

If you believe it will work out you'll see opportunities,
if you believe it won't you'll see obstacles.
DR. WAYNE W. DYER.

Synonyms for confidence are: Self-assurance, courage, self-reliance, trust, boldness, fearlessness and security. Various dictionary definitions of the word confidence are: A firm trust or faith in yourself; A faith in your ability to succeed; To be fully assured arising from reliance on oneself; A trust in your ability to deal with any situation; A sense of self-reliance. All these definitions come down to almost the same thing: **A confident person trusts that whatever situations life offers them, they will be able to deal with.**

No challenge is beyond our capability;
Every challenge promises new growth
and a measure of serenity.
KAREN CASEY / MARTHA VANCEBURG.

Since fear comes from not trusting in life or our ability to deal with a situation that we fear, one of the most powerful suggestions that we could put into our subconscious is: **"I trust in life and in my ability to deal with any situation".** The importance of this statement cannot be overestimated. Your whole life will change if you take it on board and live with trust.

This is the key to true success. Believe in yourself and feel that you are able to achieve anything that you set your mind to.

There is nothing to limit you
if you can trust in life and in your ability
to do whatever you spiritually desire.

The single, most important factor, that stops most people progressing in life is fear. Fear of failure, fear of loss, fear of rejection and above all fear of *not being able to handle* the failure, loss or rejection. A fear of making a mistake stops many people from "just going for it" but if the aim in life is to learn and develop, we can often learn just as much from making mistakes as we can from getting things right.

There is no failure
except in no longer trying.
ELBERT HUBBARD

An optimist who takes a risk probably lives by the motto "nothing ventured, nothing gained", whereas a pessimist who fears the risk of failure would probably relate more to the motto "nothing ventured, nothing lost!"

It is common sense to take a method and try it.
If it fails, admit it frankly and try another.
But above all, try something.
FRANKLIN D. ROOSEVELT.

If you are about to make a change, always try to keep uppermost in your mind the advantages, benefits and positive changes that will occur in your life.

If you are confident of your ability to handle any situation

with which you are confronted, then you will have nothing to fear.

> *Whatever you can do, or dream, you can begin it.*
> *Boldness has genius, power and magic in it.*
> GOETHE.

To start any new business venture involves a risk, to leave your home town and set up home somewhere new involves a risk, to travel the world involves a risk, to get married involves a risk, to finish a bad relationship involves a risk. **Every move that you make, and every decision that you take, involves a risk. But those who risk nearly always achieve much more in life than those who play it safe**.

> *The people who get on in this world are the*
> *people who get up and look for the circumstances they want,*
> *and, if they can't find them, make them.*
> GEORGE BERNARD SHAW.

The people who are willing to risk are those who trust in life and in their ability to deal with any situation that may arise. When you are about to take a risk you may consider winning or losing. You may think either about the improvements to your life or about how your life could worsen. Those who never dare to risk are those who dwell on all the possible dangers and problems that could come up.

> *The greatest threat to life,*
> *is to see life as a threat.*

Those who see life in this pessimistic way might say that they are being "realistic" and "playing safe", but they end up staying in a rut while always blaming the world for their unfortunate situation.

The way to guarantee failure is to maintain a strong focus on what *you don't want* to happen. **A successful person is one who imagines what they do want to happen, whereas a failure spends their time imagining what they don't want to happen.** Similarly, a coward is a person who runs away from what they fear, whereas a courageous person, may still feel the fear, but instead of running away from it they confront it and push through it. This is expressed wonderfully in the title of Susan Jeffers excellent book:

Feel the fear and do it anyway.
SUSAN JEFFERS

What is your greatest fear: To risk a change and for it to be not as you had hoped, or to stay stuck and stagnate? To begin to overcome the fear of doing something new, first do it in your imagination successfully many times. Each time that you play out the event in your mind, your subconscious will receive it as real since it can't distinguish between the imagination and reality. In other words, whenever you do this, as far as your subconscious is concerned you have already succeeded.

Any idea, thought or picture we hold in our minds will,
if it has some emotional significance for us,
produce the same reactions as if the event
or situation were actually happening.
HELLMUT W. A. KARLE.

If you want to change your life-style you may be frightened that the change may result in making you worse off than you are now and so you just stay in the rut. But if you take a risk and go for it, you discover that most of the fears that you had were just your imagination running wild.

The greatest risk of all,
is to take no risk.

Obviously, sometimes life may not go as smoothly as you'd like, but if you live with trust, things are much more likely to work out well than if you expect everything to go wrong. In addition, if things don't work out perfectly you will still learn and develop from the experience.

You're not a failure if you don't make it;
You're a success because you try.
SUSAN JEFFERS.

Taking risks is essential to make progress in life and this applies not only to major decisions such as leaving your job or moving house, but also to minor decisions such as talking to a stranger in the street or asking someone for a date.

We learn wisdom from failure much more than from success;
We often discover what will do,
by finding out what will not do;
And probably he who never made a mistake
never made a discovery.
SAMUEL SMILES.

Often the risk involves breaking away from the crowd and starting up an independent path of our own. This may mean going against convention and tradition. But the most successful people in this world are those who have the courage to break away and do what is unconventional rather than just following the norms of convention - they are the ones who become the leaders.

Successful people follow independent paths.
At some point in their lives, they break away from the
crowd and start on a path of their own.
EARL NIGHTINGALE.

When you think about how playing it safe can hold you back in life, you will realise that in many ways **it is better to take risks than to be careful!** Develop a trust in yourself and in life which will give you the confidence to take the risks necessary to make progress. Our success is limited only by our imagination and the self-confidence that we have to succeed.

The poor man has been visualising poverty,
while the rich man has been visualising wealth.

It may be argued that a man might be poor because he was born into poverty, raised with little money and got caught in the "poverty trap", however, all these factors go towards reinforcing his self-image of being a poor man, and once this image is held in the subconscious, then it is his programming that holds him in the situation and not just external circumstances. If, however, a poor man could change his self-image to one of being a rich man, and develop an unfailing confidence that life will provide him with whatever he needs to attain the wealth that he desires and expects, then, through his positive thoughts, beliefs, expectations and actions he will climb out of poverty into the wealthy position that he has been visualising.

*Why build
a shack
for yourself in
your imagination,
when you could build
a palace?*

The Technique
Of
Self-Suggestion

The Technique Of Self-Suggestion

To believe a thing is impossible is to make it so.
FRENCH PROVERB.

If someone makes the statement: "I'm not the kind of person who does that!" or "But I just can't see myself doing that!" then they are creating their reality by the fact that that is what they believe. But, if they change their self-image and they can begin to see themselves engaging in the particular activity, then they will very soon discover that it is actually within their capability.

One of the most destructive thoughts that you can have to stop you getting on in life is: "I can't do that". There is a very well-known proverb that says: "*There's no such word as can't!*" I don't particularly like the way that this is expressed, since this word obviously exists, but it is true that as soon as your subconscious registers the word "can't" regarding your abilities, then obviously.....you can't! **If you believe that you can't do something then you are right,** because the self-doubt will stop you creating the conditions necessary to achieve whatever it is that you believe that you can't do. Conversely, **if you believe that you can do something then you are right also,** because the belief will motivate you into action to set up the conditions to make it happen. Obvious really isn't it?

You are what you are and where you are because of the way you think and what you believe about yourself.

It is our internal programming, that, through our thoughts and beliefs, creates our actions and hence influences the reactions of everyone with whom we interact.

Our personal environment is of our own making - our consciousness creates our circumstances. When we curse the world or other people for "unfortunate" events, we are transmitting to our subconscious that we are helpless victims of life. Complaining about life also has the effect that when the words we speak are registered by our subconscious they act as negative suggestions to create the state which we are complaining about. What we are really saying is "I have no control, neither on the events nor on how I see the events". However, the truth is that, **we have as much control over our lives as we believe we have.** This is an extremely empowering statement, think about it carefully before you read on.

So, if we believe that we have no control over our lives and that it is all due to external events, then we are right. But, if we believe that we have full control over our lives and that we are the creators of our circumstances then we are still right. It is worth repeating that very important statement, here it is again:

We have as much control over our lives
as we believe we have.

WHAT IS SELF-SUGGESTION?

The technique of self-suggestion basically involves repeating to yourself a verbal suggestion whilst holding a corresponding positive image in your mind. For the technique to work it is important that the positive messages don't just remain in your mind, but penetrate into the subconscious, since it is from here that they will have their greatest effect. A suggestion which remains at the level of your mind may have some effect, but **a suggestion which penetrates into the subconscious will have astounding effects.**

But how can you make contact with the subconscious? The way to get suggestions through to the subconscious is to change your state of consciousness, this can be done in two ways:

1)   By going into a state of deep relaxation.
2)   By working yourself up into a highly emotional state. (See page 134).

Other terms that are sometimes used in place of self-suggestion, are auto-suggestion and self-hypnosis, the main difference being that these processes necessitate an altered state of consciousness. Self-suggestion, can, if you prefer, be carried out in a normal state of consciousness, if the suggestion is repeated enough times. In this context we may use the term "affirmation" to describe the statement that we are repeating.

In this book I will use the term self-suggestion in the broad sense of being applied in any state of consciousness. For example, if while walking along the road you repeat an affirmation such as "I am feeling dynamically energetic", the term self-suggestion can be used, whereas if you were to repeat it while lying on your bed relaxing, it might be more appropriate to use the term self-hypnosis. The job of a hypnotherapist is to help you to enter a deep state of relaxation and then implant positive, empowering suggestions into the subconscious.

The technique of self-suggestion is primarily one of verbalisation, that is, repeating words to yourself in your mind. But for these verbal suggestions to have their maximum effect they need to be enhanced by using visualisation techniques, that is, forming mental pictures within your imagination. When you form a suggestion and say it to yourself, the words you say are very important, but even more important are the images and feelings that accompany the words. It is very important to remember that **if the visual image is in conflict with the verbal suggestion then the image wins**, this is the reason why "will power" sometimes fails. If for example you tell yourself: "I am an energetic, hard-working person", but your self-image is that you are a lethargic, lazy person then the suggestion will have very little effect. If, however, while making the positive suggestion in a relaxed state, you visualise yourself how you would like to be - in a good mood, positive, smiling and full of energy, and you hold this image of yourself while repeating the suggestion, then *it will work*. It would be better to tell yourself that you are a failure but picture yourself as a success, than to tell yourself that you are a success and picture yourself as a failure. Obviously though, neither of these are very sensible, what is most beneficial is to tell yourself that you are a great success while holding a corresponding image in your mind.

If we tell ourselves enough times that we are really weak, or that we get ill very easily, or that we are fed-up with life, then we will eventually make it come true. How quickly this happens depends on the link between the mind and the subconscious. If we want to make positive suggestions which have a profound effect on our lives we have to find a way of putting the censor or guard to sleep (see page 20), and this is the purpose of going into a deep state of relaxation.

In using the technique of self-suggestion the positive suggestions that you tell yourself, could be regarding any aspect of your life - your health, your emotional state, your memory, your confidence, how you feel about life, what you really want to achieve, or whatever.

Suppose, for example, you want to give up eating sweets, or other sugary foods, and you tell yourself while walking along the street: "From now on I'm never going to have another sweet", then that afternoon or the next day you are offered one, and you find yourself automatically accepting it. What happened? Well it could have been two things, one is that you didn't truly believe that you would be successful due to a strong image of failure. Someone may tell themselves that they are not going to eat cream cakes anymore, while their image is of themselves as a person who just can't resist, and therefore, they can't resist. Similarly, someone may tell themselves that they are going to give up smoking but their self-image is one of a smoker who just can't give up, and so they can't give up! The second and main reason for failing to resist the sweets is that the suggestion didn't get through to the subconscious where it has it's most powerful effect.

If, while suggesting to yourself: "I no longer eat sweets and cakes", you first go into a deep state of relaxation, the suggestion will have much more chance of penetrating into the subconscious, and your resistance to these food products is then very likely to increase considerably. In addition, if the suggestion is reinforced by visualising yourself as a person who finds it easy to resist, then you are even more likely to achieve your objective.

Self-suggestion will work for almost anyone. The technique will almost certainly work for you if *any of the following* apply to you:

1)   You are well motivated to make a change.
2)   You have a reasonable imagination.
3)   You sometimes lie awake at night worrying.
4)   You are an open-minded person.
5)   You believe in the power of your mind.
6)   You daydream a lot (daydreaming is a kind of trance state).

It may not be the ideal technique for you if you don't believe that you have access to your subconscious, or if you refuse to believe that it could work. You may also find it difficult if you have absolutely no imagination or creative ability, and if you never daydream or worry about the future.

If you daydream a lot, then you will find this technique a very powerful one for you. Next time you go into a daydream let positive thoughts and images run through your mind. If you do this, you will notice immediately a change of feeling within you as you come out of the daydream. This is a mild form of hypnotherapy, but to learn the technique properly there are certain rules that I shall soon explain, that you need to keep in mind regarding the way you word your suggestions.

Since the level of success that you achieve will be greatly determined by how confident you feel about being able to use this technique to change your life, if you intend to make use of it, I would advise you to start by repeating the following preliminary suggestion:

I am confident that I am able to use the technique of self-suggestion to achieve anything that I want to achieve in life.

ARE OUR TRUTHS TRUE?

I know I'm not seeing things as they are,
I'm seeing things as I am.
LAUREL LEE.

It is a fact that we all see things and interpret things according to the way we think and what we already believe - this depends on both our level of consciousness and on previous conditioning. If we have fixed, strong, unchangeable beliefs, then when a new idea comes to us, instead of truly listening we are just comparing it with what we already believe so that we can either agree or disagree.

*The ego is a self-justifying historian which
seeks only that information that agrees with it,
rewrites history when it needs to,
and does not even see the evidence that threatens it.*
ANTHONY G. GREENWALD.

There are many negative beliefs that we have, that we see as "truths", which may be just beliefs which we have picked up as a result of negative suggestion. These beliefs are possible to change, if the desire to change them is present. All through our childhood we are "hypnotised" with countless negative suggestions by hearing them over and over again. For example, you may have heard your parents saying things like: "She is a very shy girl", "He doesn't like going to bed", "She really needs her sleep", "He gets colds very easily", and so on. Or, they may have told you directly: "you are a very naughty girl", "you silly boy", "you shouldn't be so lazy". All these can have a harmful effect if the suggestions penetrate into the subconscious. Almost every human being, while growing up, is subjected to ideas like these which are not beneficial to their development.

Below, I have written just a few examples of the type of negative suggestions that we can hold on to as truths, without realising that they are just suggestions:

Are any of these true for you?
1)   I need at least 8 hours sleep every night.
2)   I'm always irritable in the morning.
3)   I have always had trouble getting to sleep.
4)   My concentration span is very short.
5)   I have always been very shy.
6)   I have a terrible memory.
7)   The rain depresses me.
8)   I have very little will-power.

9)   I get ill very easily.
10)   The slightest draught gives me a sore throat.
11)   I am a worrier.
12)   I always have bad luck.
13)   I'm not very good at sports.
14)   I have never been good at maths.
15)   I'm not very clever.
16)   I'm not very creative
17)   I have a weak stomach.
18)   I can never eat in the morning.
19)   If I eat after 8.00pm I can't sleep.
20)   I can't...............

These create the reality that we live. If any of these are true for you, then you may have always seen them as "innate, unchangeable characteristics", and you may have said: "That's just the way I am!" However, the fact is that all the above statements are not "truths", but simply beliefs which have come about as a result of negative suggestion during your up-bringing. This is very good news, because fortunately, all suggestions are reversible. So, even if you have always believed that you are always irritable in the morning, it is possible to change your belief, and of course your reality, to: "I always feel good in the morning". All that you have to do is suggest this to yourself every day until it penetrates into your subconscious and subsequently you will become a person who always feels good in the morning.

A few other, even more incredible, examples of "truths" which can have a profound effect on you, and yet may simply be the result of suggestion are:

1)   I suffer with my back.
2)   My health has never been good.
3)   I only have to look at food to put on weight.

4)   My eyesight is terrible

5)   I am hyperactive by nature.

You may think that these examples are taking the power of belief a bit too far, however, as I will soon explain, our health, our fitness, and even our metabolic rate is affected by our subconscious programming, which, in turn, is affected by our thoughts, opinions and beliefs.

We may, without realising it, be programming ourselves with negative suggestions, because this is the way that we got used to being spoken to throughout our childhood. Many of our beliefs are so deeply engrained that it is difficult to let go of them unless we make a conscious decision to. This can only happen when we come to realise that our beliefs are not "truths" but just opinions.

Do you tell yourself off, more often for some aspect of your character or behaviour, than tell yourself well done? If you do, then it is probably because of what you got used to hearing while you were growing up. It is important to realise that the way you "talk to yourself" can affect your whole outlook on life.

Fortunately, all suggestions are reversible, so, if throughout childhood you were continually called lazy, shy, stupid, weak or if you were taught by ridicule and therefore have a negative self-image, you are now in the position to change this self-image. However, it isn't very likely to change overnight, (although it could if you believed that it could!). Since the negativity was implanted through repetition, the opposite positive suggestions have to be implanted and repeated as many times as is necessary to counteract and eventually to eliminate the effects of the negative suggestions that you were subjected to. The stronger the negativity is, the more work that is required to reverse it.

You may want to hold onto your truths vehemently, expressing something like: "But *I know* that a draught *does* give me a sore throat and this isn't just my imagination, it *is* the effect of the draught not of negative suggestion". Well I would agree with this *if* you have just spent a few hours talking to someone with a streaming cold, coughing all over you, *and* you spent so long in the draught that it lowered your internal body temperature. But if you simply sat in a draught for one minute and then got a sore throat then this surely *is* the result of suggestion. **The subconscious has the power to give you a sore throat in seconds,** all that is necessary is a trigger which activates the negative suggestion that has been programmed into your subconscious. I recently met a man who said: "I am so sensitive to draughts that if I sit in a slight movement of air for a few seconds, I will start to sneeze". The fact that he could actually sneeze whenever he was in a slight draught illustrates well, the power of the subconscious to create what we believe. In reality a draught can only be a problem in two instances - either if it lowers the internal body temperature, (not just the surface temperature of the skin), or if we are continually in a slight draught for many years. (Or maybe this is my own limiting belief which creates my own reality!)

We all have destructive beliefs which are not serving us in any way. It is possible that if, while reading this, you haven't ever heard any beliefs of the type I have been describing, you may be thinking: "What nonsense! If someone can believe something so crazy they can't be very intelligent - how can anyone believe that a movement of air can cause a sore throat or a cold?" But instead of judging others for their "crazy" beliefs, which doesn't help anyone, you could, through an increased awareness, try to discover your own negative conditioning so that you can form a belief system that serves you. Since our beliefs create our reality, it is important for us to examine our own beliefs and ask the question: "Is this belief good for me?" Many of the beliefs that we will need to question, we may not even think are "beliefs" but may see as "facts". However, if we have an open mind we will begin to see that there are certain beliefs that we might hold simply because we have heard them stated so many times. Everyone has their own "crazy" conditioned beliefs and we will be in a much healthier position if, instead of judging others we do everything we can to try to get to know our own. This isn't as easy as it sounds, it requires a great deal of openness, a persistent effort, and a willingness to accept that we might be wrong in what we already believe, (this is the greatest challenge for many people). The longer that we hold onto destructive, self-sabotaging beliefs, the more deep-seated they become. In this situation, awareness and a strong desire to release the beliefs are required if we are to be healed from their consequences.

Self-analysis of our own conditioned beliefs becomes even more challenging when we realise that the beliefs that we most need to release are those which are so deeply engrained that we are not even aware of their existence - these are the ideas and opinions that we may have heard and taken on board from the time that we started to walk and talk. These are the beliefs that we see as "truths", and are the most difficult to release, even if they are not serving us.

It is time to ask ourselves whether many of the negative thoughts and feelings that we have about life in general, are just a result of negative conditioning, rather than from some intrinsic, unpleasant properties of life itself. If we are going to hold on to illogical truths for ourselves, then we might as well set them up to be helpful truths.

Make sure that what you believe
serves you well.

RELEASE DESTRUCTIVE BELIEFS

We all have both personal beliefs and cultural beliefs. Our personal beliefs are not static - as they are continually challenged we adjust them in the light of new information. However, our cultural beliefs are less often challenged unless we step out of the culture in which we were brought up and consider a totally different set of beliefs. If we stay within our own culture, we can live our whole life without ever once questioning whether our "truths" might not be true after all.

A question that I find very interesting is this: "If two separate cultures have opposing beliefs then how can we possibly know who is right? For example, if in one country everyone believes that a certain food is unhealthy, while in another country everyone believes that it is good for you, how can we know who is right? You may answer: "Eat it and find out!" But, if you believe in the power of your mind, you will realise that this is no solution because those who believe that it is bad for them may become sick after eating it, while those who believe that it is good, will feel fine. This is especially true if the belief permeates the whole of society. It is certainly true that if while eating something you think to yourself: "Oh dear, I shouldn't be eating this, I know it's going to give me a stomach ache", then it almost certainly will! So, the answer to the question "If two separate cultures have opposing beliefs then how can we possibly know who is right? is: "They are both right, because **we create our reality by what we believe.**" This point confirms what I expressed previously, that it is very important to reassess what we believe so that **we can hold on to the beliefs that serve us and let go of those that don't.**

The belief that something is bad for you
makes it bad for you.

I once knew a Spanish girl who believed that having a bath or shower while she was having her monthly periods could be very dangerous. She thought that it can stop the period and cause major problems within the uterine system. *This was her truth*, she said that she had heard it all her life and *"everyone is aware of the dangers"*. I asked my sisters and several other women about this and they said that they have never heard such nonsense. She was shocked to discover that *they didn't know* about this. I tried to explain to her that it is just a myth, an "old wives tale", passed down from generation to generation probably in the area where she lived (or possibly just within her family), but she found it very difficult to let go of her "truth" since she had heard it ever since she was very young. It required medical confirmation of the falseness of the belief and plenty of positive suggestion before she came to the point where she could accept that it might not be dangerous. It took a long time before she felt relaxed enough to have a shower during her periods without worrying. Because of the power of the subconscious, it is possible that if she did have a shower, while believing that it is dangerous, then it could have had a harmful effect, thus reinforcing her "truth". I think that this is how people become convinced of "false truths", since they may test what they believe, and, if they believe it strongly enough the belief is confirmed to be true. In fact, this only goes to confirm the immense power that we have within us to create our reality.

Nothing is good or bad - thinking makes it so.
WILLIAM SHAKESPEARE.

REPROGRAMMING THE SUBCONSCIOUS

Every statement which has been impressed upon the subconscious has a profound effect on our lives. Negative beliefs can have an adverse effect on our body, our health, our behaviour, our self-image and the way we socially interact. For this reason, we will receive enormous benefit if we can eliminate harmful, negative statements from the subconscious and replace them with positive beliefs that will enhance our lives.

Much of the information contained in the subconscious was pre-programmed before birth, but much is conditioned information, and it is this which can cause problems if the conditioning is negative. I like to compare this programming of negative information into the subconscious with the corruption of a well-written computer programme by a virus. Without the virus, the programme functions perfectly, but once the virus is present, all sorts of things can go wrong - our subconscious is very much like this - babies are born with perfect programming, but through negative suggestion the subconscious becomes corrupted. It is even possible that ageing occurs because of the inevitable corruption of the subconscious programming - cells make mistakes as they divide because the negative conditioning that we are subjected to throughout life acts like a computer virus - the programme that tells the cells how to divide becomes more and more corrupted as the years go by.

In babies, the subconscious works in a very efficient, harmonious way to control the bodily processes, but then, as the child grows, suggestions start impinging onto the subconscious which can change the natural programming causing problems in the natural working of the body. For example, there are very few babies, if any, who would be bothered about drinking warm water, but there are many adults who find warm water disgusting. This is clearly a result of conditioning, some have very strong conditioning in this way and I have even heard one person express that drinking warm water makes them feel like vomiting - this is obviously the result of negative suggestion.

Because babies look so helpless and vulnerable many people think that they are weak and sensitive, but this is definitely not the case. It is true that babies are totally dependent on the adults around them for their survival but they are very resilient, tough little creatures, and I believe that this is mainly due to the fact that their subconscious programming is totally pure and uncorrupted and therefore working at maximum efficiency. For example, if an adult and a baby were both left to die in some horrible situation then the adult is much more likely to die first. This is due, primarily, to the negative effects upon the system of worry, fear and anger, which will affect the adult but not the baby. In September 1985 a huge earthquake hit Mexico city and its maternity hospital was totally destroyed. Rescue workers found over 50 new born babies in the rubble covered in dirt, dust and grime but still alive. There are many stories of car crashes where every occupant was killed except the baby. Recently I heard a story of a hurricane which tore through a house killing every family member and yet the baby was found almost one kilometre away unharmed.

So, although babies appear to be very delicate, vulnerable little creatures they are in many ways tougher than adults. It is theoretically possible that this durability and resilience can be maintained and developed whilst growing up if negative conditioning is avoided. Unfortunately, in practice, this isn't very easily achievable because someone could only be reared without negativity if all the adults in their environment were free of negativity.

As we become more aware of the part that our subconscious programming plays in creating our health and happiness, we become more watchful of what we tell ourselves and those around us, so that we can minimise the harmful effects of negative suggestions.

RULES FOR SUGGESTION

It is possible that even if you are relaxed the suggestion still may not work, since the way that you form the suggestion is very important. Below are guidelines on how to form a powerful suggestion:

1)   **Suggestions should always be in the present tense.**
E.g. "I am feeling really confident" not "I am soon going to be a confident person". If the suggestions are voiced in future tense then they always remain out of your grasp. The subconscious takes every word literally, it doesn't reason in the same way that the mind does. For the subconscious it is true that *tomorrow never comes.* If you say "tomorrow I will be successful" it will forever remain as tomorrow.

Many people who start to use the technique of self-suggestion, don't like to use the present tense because they argue something like this: "What is the point of telling myself that I am feeling good about something or that I am feeling confident, if I know that it is a lie?" Well, although our *mind* may believe it is a lie, our subconscious certainly doesn't, it listens to everything that it is told, and it is the subconscious that has the power to create the reality that we experience.

If you still feel very resistant to affirming in the present tense, you can phrase your suggestions in such a way that you are stating that you will very soon become how you want to become, but the change has started now. E.g. "Every day I am becoming more confident".

2)   **Suggestions should always be voiced in the positive.**
E.g. "I am a happy, relaxed person", and not "I am no longer a miserable, tense person". This is a very important rule since we tend to form images according to the "energetic" words within

the suggestion and the words "miserable" and "tense" are more penetrating to the subconscious than the words "no longer". Also if I tell you now NOT to think about a Giraffe, what happens?

If you are a bit of a rebel it is possible that you instantly thought of a lion or some other animal but the majority of people would not be able to help themselves thinking about a giraffe. If your problem is feeling tired all the time you should say: "I always feel full of energy" and not "I am not tired all the time". This is true also of our lives in general. We should try to focus all our attention on what we want, not on what we don't want, in other words, **live your life to maximise happiness, not to minimise misery.**

3) **Don't refer to past conditions.**
E.g. It is wrong to say: "I am more relaxed than I used to be". The image of how you have been is stronger than the image of how you wish to be.

4) **Use powerful words.**
Use words that convey a lot of meaning and feeling, such as fantastic, vibrant, dynamic, ecstatic, super, wonderful, and so on.

5) **Be specific and realistic.**
Don't try to make ten changes to your life all at once. E.g. I am now a happy, healthy, relaxed, energetic, patient, enthusiastic, confident, loving, open, successful person. You can become all of these, but concentrate on just one aspect of your life to work on or one quality to develop at any one time. Also, so that you can build up confidence in the technique make your first attempts at trying to change your life through self-suggestion something that will impress you, but not too difficult.

6)   **The suggestion should not be negligent of other peoples feelings.**

If it is totally inconsiderate to those around you, then the principles of self-suggestion may be interrupted by feelings of guilt. Developing power over your own life, must still take into consideration an overview that makes certain that no harm or suffering will be caused to anyone else. E.g. "I will win whatever it takes" is not a good suggestion because the "whatever" within the suggestion could include any type of behaviour.

7)   **Your suggestions should never involve trying to change someone else.**

You can only work on yourself and in so doing, your environment and those around you will adjust as you change. E.g. don't suggest: "my children are starting to respect me more and behave better with me", because this is requiring them to change. Instead suggest: "I take a sincere interest in my children, and give them all the love, attention and encouragement that they deserve", then form a visual image of yourself interacting pleasantly with them. Clearly, as soon as your behaviour towards your children changes, their responses will automatically change. This realisation enables you to take responsibility for your interactions so that you can be in a position of power rather than helplessness.

8)   **Form a mental image which is consistent with the suggestion.**

If you are over-sensitive to the cold and you want to develop your resistance to it, you may use a suggestion such as: "I now have a good resistance to the cold", while repeating this suggestion you could imagine yourself in situations which are consistent with the suggestion, such as walking through the park in winter enjoying the cold air or standing at a bus stop, while smiling, with a lovely fresh wind blowing against your face.

Sometimes you might have to make exceptions to some of the above rules, such as not always expressing in the positive. There is no need to worry about this since they are only guidelines and not hard and fast rules. For example, suppose that you wanted to increase your tolerance to pain. There is no obvious word which is the opposite to pain so the suggestion could be something like: "Pain just doesn't bother me anymore, I am able to handle it with ease", this suggestion, if repeated enough times will have a positive effect. However, if you can possibly avoid the use of the word pain in what you want to say it is preferable. It is usually possible to find a way of expressing in the positive, the question to ask yourself is: "what is the state I am trying to move towards?" For example, if you suffer from painful arthritic joints you could suggest something like: "My knees feel healthy and comfortable". This is more likely to be effective than "The pain in my knees is now disappearing".

Some people say that suggestions have their most powerful effect when they are written down. Although I am not 100% in agreement with this, I think that writing down a suggestion several times can definitely have a powerful effect, especially if you are in the state of mind to allow suggestions to penetrate into the subconscious.

If you are conscientious and are willing to devote a little extra time to your self-development, the following system can have excellent results:

1)   Write down the suggestion.

2)   Form a visual image in your mind which is consistent with the suggestion.

3)   Read the suggestion out loud three times while holding the positive image in your mind.

4) Write it down again, then repeat steps 2 and 3.

5) Relax for a short while. Now hold the image in your mind and repeat the positive suggestion.

6) Go for a walk, or go and sit in a beautiful place while holding the positive thoughts in your mind.

In addition to the above steps, repeat the suggestion to yourself at any odd moments, such as while washing-up, cutting the grass, brushing your teeth, walking along the street, or driving your car. The effect is cumulative, that is, the more times that you repeat the suggestion, the more powerful will be its effect.

It can be particularly powerful if you repeat positive suggestions while looking into a mirror, making eye contact with yourself. Sometimes saying a positive suggestion out loud can have a far greater effect than just thinking it. Try experimenting with this yourself, to discover what is most effective for you. Some like to chant their suggestion in a monotone like a priest's singing, while others repeat it, starting off out loud and then continually repeating the suggestion while getting lower and lower until they are repeating the suggestion silently in their mind, (this is similar to meditating on a mantra).

LEARNING TO RELAX

The importance of relaxation cannot be over-estimated, the more often you relax, the healthier you will become. The ability to deeply relax at regular intervals will improve a whole range of physical and mental processes including many of those listed above. If a person finds it difficult to relax and lives in a constant state of tension, this will have negative consequences on every facet of their life, such as constant tiredness and fatigue, poor health and lack of inner peace. It has been shown that the body's efficiency, In terms of repair and regeneration, increases while the brain is generating alpha waves. If you relax regularly you will have more vitality, you will sleep better, and you will wake up feeling more refreshed. This is apart from the enormous good that the positive self-suggestions can do while you are in a deep state of relaxation. **The ability to relax is invaluable.** If you can relax deeply twice a day for 15 minutes the benefits will astound you.

EFFORTLESS EFFORT

What you must remember when engaging in any kind of activity which involves becoming more in harmony with yourself such as relaxing, meditating or going to sleep, is **don't try too hard.** Consider an insomniac who is trying to get to sleep, the harder they try the more trouble they have. Sometimes the harder you try to do something the harder it becomes, and then as soon as you stop trying it just happens. Getting to sleep is one example of this and going into a trance state is another.

The key to relaxing deeply is to just let go. Let go of your tensions, let go of your worries, let go of your problems, let go of your negativity. While you are starting to relax don't tell yourself: "Oh, I'm probably doing this wrong", just let yourself be. Don't criticise, don't judge, don't condemn, just accept what you're doing and slowly and peacefully go through the relaxation procedure in an enjoyable way.

Don't try to force anything. Let life be a deep let-go.
See God opening millions of flowers
everyday without forcing the buds.
SHREE RAJNEESH.

The practice of yoga exercises follows the same rules of "effortless effort", you should never force yourself to stretch, because if you do, your body will react to this by tensing up, since every action has an equal and opposite reaction. The stretching should by done by *effortlessly* extending your body into the various positions.

> *That the yielding conquers the resistant*
> *and the soft conquers the hard,*
> *is a fact known by all but utilised by none.*
> LAO TZU.

STATES OF RELAXATION

There are various states of relaxation that are reflected by the activity of the brain. If the brain waves of subjects in various states of relaxation are observed using a special instrument called an electroencephalogram it can be seen that the frequency of these waves change as someone moves from a normal waking state into deep relaxation. The frequency ranges, measured in cycles per second (cyc/s), are given names using the letters of the Greek alphabet as shown below:

Normal waking state - Beta waves, 14 cyc/s or more.
Day dreaming, resting - Alpha waves, 8 - 13 cyc/s.
Trance state, meditative state or sleep - Theta waves, 5 - 7 cyc/s.
Deep sleep - Delta, less than 5 cyc/s.

While you are in the beta state, suggestions may have some difficulty getting through to the subconscious, but in the more relaxed states of alpha and theta they get through much more easily. The relaxation technique that you are going to learn will get you into the alpha state very easily, and in this state the censor or "guard" is lulled and the channel is open to allow suggestions through to your subconscious. In the alpha state you are very relaxed but still alert and fully conscious of everything that is going on around you - this is the ideal state to be in to practice the technique of self-suggestion. In the theta state the censor is down, and, at this time, someone else such as a hypnotherapist can programme positive suggestions into your subconscious.

You can still perform self-suggestion if you are not relaxed but the speed with which it takes affect increases the more relaxed you are. The deeper the state of relaxation the greater is the effect of the positive suggestions, and the less repetition that is required. This is illustrated below:

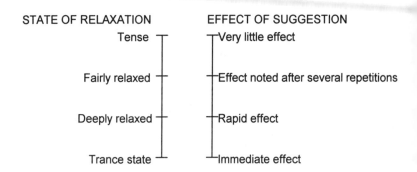

STATE OF RELAXATION

Tense

Fairly relaxed

Deeply relaxed

Trance state

EFFECT OF SUGGESTION

Very little effect

Effect noted after several repetitions

Rapid effect

Immediate effect

THE RELAXATION TECHNIQUE

There are many different methods that you can use to get into a deep state of relaxation, but I am going to focus here mainly on a particular type of breathing technique. **Breathing is one of the few bodily processes that is under both conscious and subconscious control** and therefore gives us a way of creating a bridge to the subconscious that can enable reprogramming to occur during relaxation.

You can practice the relaxation sessions at any time of the day, but in the beginning while you are learning the technique the best times are either just after waking up in the morning or last thing at night. It is important to realise that once you get the basic idea of how to relax and use self-suggestion techniques, you can do it at anytime, wherever you may be.

Before you begin the relaxation technique you can, if you like, prepare a nice atmosphere to associate with your relaxation sessions. For example, if you like the smell of incense you can light some for a few minutes just before you begin to relax, or you can use relaxing music. Before getting into your relaxation position you should first decide on a specific suggestion that you are going to repeat, or on a specific aspect of your character or behaviour that you want to work on. Now, when you have the atmosphere that you want, carry out the following steps:

- Get into a position that you find comfortable which will enable you to relax while remaining conscious, there is no specific position that you should be in as long as you don't fall asleep. (Although if this happens, just accept it, since it might be just what your body needs at that particular time.) You could sit cross-legged, lie on the bed, lie on the floor, sit in your armchair, whatever you prefer, the important thing is that you are comfortable.

- Close your eyes and take two or three deep breaths. Visualise the air not as an invisible substance but as a flowing, white or golden light. Now, as you breathe, just imagine the air flowing through your body filling you with energy. Imagine the air glowing with a bright, radiant energy and as you breathe let this energy penetrate to every cell of your body.

- As you breathe imagine this energised air entering your arteries and veins making you feel so good. Visualise your whole body bathed in this golden energy. Imagine each breath feeding you with energy making you feel more connected to everything. You are starting to feel wonderfully energised.

- Now, continue breathing, and, as you breathe, imagine this life-giving energy entering each body part in turn starting from your feet, then your legs, your groin, your trunk, your arms and your head. Each time you take a breath, focus on a body part and feel the life-energy entering it to produce a wonderful sensation of relaxation.

- You are now going to enter into a deeper state of relaxation and make contact with your subconscious. Imagine a staircase with 20 stairs. You are at the top and as you count down from 20 to 1 you will descend the staircase and go deeper and deeper into relaxation. It is helpful, but not essential, if you can synchronise walking down the stairs with your breathing. Each time you exhale, take one step down and count 20, 19, 18, and so on, until you reach the base on the count of 1.

- At the bottom of the stairs you will find a door to a room that represents your subconscious. There is a very comfortable couch or armchair in this room, go over to it and make yourself comfortable. As you sit comfortably in this imaginary seat you will sink deeper and deeper into a wonderful state of relaxation.

- When you are fully relaxed, just sit quietly for a minute allowing your mind to do whatever it wants before you start telling yourself positive self-suggestions.

By this stage you will be feeling deeply relaxed and your brain will be producing alpha waves. Suggestions can now have a profound effect because they are able to get through to your subconscious.

Just before starting your suggestion there is a very useful technique to make your brain waves slow down even more. With your eyes closed try to look at the inside of your forehead - in other words rotate your eyes up at an angle of about 30 degrees - after a few seconds relax them again and take a deep breath. Repeat this two or three times, you will feel a strange but wonderful sensation as you go into a deeper state of relaxation. Obviously, you don't need to do the eye movement if it doesn't help to make you feel good, only do it if it is comfortable.

Now, tell yourself something like: "Each time I relax like this I will find it more pleasant and reach deeper and deeper states of relaxation" or "I am successfully mastering this technique of relaxation and I am sure that it is good for me". Try to avoid thinking things like: "Oh dear, I'm not doing this right, I don't think I am going to be able to get the hang of this." Always think of yourself as successful, especially while in a state of relaxation.

When you are feeling as relaxed as you can get, you are ready to make your suggestion in the way that I shall explain in the next section. While you are in this deep state of relaxation, before coming back to "normal", you can make use of this relaxation session to programme into your subconscious various reinforcement suggestions to strengthen your resolve such as:

1)   Each time I repeat this technique I am going to enter into a deeper and deeper state of relaxation, and find that the suggestions have a stronger effect.

2)   When I say the words: "I am a success" I will feel a surge of energy go through me which will enable me to do anything that I need to do to improve my life.

As an extension to this relaxation exercise, you can, if you wish, while focusing on each body part in turn, send them positive, loving feelings as you breathe in and out. This is known to have a highly beneficial effect on the health. One of the most health enhancing techniques that you can engage in, is to practice loving your body. The power of suggestion is considerable if we can discover ways of telling our bodies how to improve without being critical. If we lovingly take care of anything that lives, from a flower to our own waistline it *must* respond to some degree. If we leave our body to "just get on with it", it will respond to the ingrained knowledge or conditioning that at certain stages in our life it will create extra fatty tissue (middle age spread), weak joints, saggy bits, slower responses, poor circulation, and so on. But given the correct attention and tender loving care, it can be totally unaware that it should be acquiring "age symptoms", and respond much more to how you want it to be on every level.

COMING OUT OF RELAXATION
To come out of the relaxation you could count to five saying to yourself something like:

One, ah that was a wonderful relaxation session, I feel fantastic.

Two, *(bring a smile to your face)* I'm starting to wake up now, but as I come back to normal I will continue to feel wonderful.

Three, *(start to wiggle your fingers and toes now)* I'm feeling almost awake now, but I still feel wonderfully relaxed.

Four, *(have a stretch)*, I feel wide awake and I'm going to continue the day with the same positive feeling as I have now.

Five, *(open your eyes)* ah, that was good, I'm going to repeat that again in the next day or so.

MAKING YOUR SUGGESTION

While you are in a relaxed state you will be ready to carry out the verbal suggestion, there are two ways in which you can do this:

1)   If the suggestion is short and if you remember it, repeat it to yourself several times. E.g. "I am a creative, artistic person".

2)   If the suggestion is more than about 10 words, you could give it a title which holds for you all the meaning that is contained within the suggestion. You then only need to repeat the title to yourself several times while you are relaxed.

For example: If the suggestion is for overcoming feelings of inferiority, you could use a suggestion like:

SUPER-CONFIDENT

I am a confident, attractive, easy-going person. I feel relaxed in any social situation. I have trust in myself and in my ability to deal with any situation that confronts me and I can achieve anything that I set my mind to.

Before relaxing, read the suggestion to yourself several times so that the title holds all the meaning for you that the suggestion contains, then when you are deeply relaxed you will only need to repeat the title to yourself: "I am a super-confident person".

If you have the problem of always feeling tired you could write out a suggestion something like the following:

DYNAMICALLY ENERGETIC

I am a healthy, strong person, full of energy and vitality. I always wake up feeling wonderfully refreshed and full of life, and still feel good at the end of a busy day.

This can be used in the same way as the previous suggestion. Read it several times, and then while relaxing you will only need to repeat to yourself: "I feel dynamically energetic" several times while holding in your mind a corresponding visual image of yourself.

CLASSICAL CONDITIONING

It can be very valuable, while in a deeply relaxed state, to programme into your subconscious a conditioned response such as "When I am in normal waking consciousness, all I need to do is touch my earlobe or my chin, say the word "relax", and I will immediately feel wonderfully relaxed". This is an example of a programmed or conditioned response, such as that discovered years ago by a psychologist called Pavlov while carrying out experiments with his Dogs. He rang a bell every time he presented his dogs with food - as soon as he did this they showed excitement and would salivate in anticipation of the treat to come. After a while the dogs would respond in a similar way to the ring of the bell on its own even when no food was presented, because they had learnt to associate the ringing with food. We have many conditioned responses like this ourselves. For example some people panic at the sight of a spider or to the sound of a dentist's drill. Research has also shown that if, for example, we are subjected to a certain smell at the same time as being given a stressful task which invokes the stress response, then after a while the stress response can be invoked by the smell alone. Conversely, if we associate the smell of incense with a relaxing atmosphere due to always smelling it in a church, chapel, ashram, or other relaxing environment, then it is possibly due to this conditioned association that the smell could have a relaxing effect on our physiology. In a similar way, if, every time we feel relaxed, we touch our ear-lobe and associate this with a feeling of deep relaxation, and we also programme into our subconscious that this will cause us to deeply relax and think more clearly, then at any future moment we can go very quickly into a relaxed state simply by touching our ear-lobe. Obviously, this effect can be induced by whatever we believe can induce it, for example rubbing your chin, scratching your head, loosely closing your hand, or, as is recommended in many eastern practices, simply putting your finger and thumb together.

WHEN TO PRACTICE SELF-SUGGESTION

Even though I have put considerable emphasis on the importance of relaxation, you shouldn't think that this means that it is not worth suggesting something to yourself while, for example, you are just walking along the street. It is well worth it, since every thought that goes through your mind is important and even one single positive suggestion is better than nothing.

Excellent opportunities to repeat suggestions to yourself occur while waiting for a bus or while driving, and, if repeated enough times they do get through to the subconscious even if you are not deeply relaxed. It is encouraging to realise that every bit of work that you do on your own self-development is cumulative - no effort is wasted. Every time you relax, every time you visualise yourself as a success, every time you have positive thoughts of yourself, you are moving in the direction of greater control over your life.

There are two times of day when it is particularly important what you say to yourself and what images you allow to go through your mind. These times are when you are waking up in the morning and when you are going to sleep at night; at these times your brain is in the alpha state and the channel to the subconscious is open. So, if you wake up saying to yourself: "Oh dear, another tough day coming up, I bet the weather is horrible, I'm dreading going to work", then it is fairly clear how you are programming your day, and it will probably turn out to be just as bad as you thought it would.

Every morning as you wake up, tell yourself something nice, such as: "This is the start of another wonderful day, I am so lucky to be healthy, I have many good people around me in my life, I am really happy". It might be better for you, if, instead of using the exact suggestions that I have included in this book, you write out and memorise statements of your own which are meaningful to you and which represent the reality that you want to create.

To finish the day, it is important to be as positive as you possibly can. If you go to sleep thinking about how tough life is, or how you would love to change your job but you can't, then that is the reality that you are creating. When you get into bed at the end of the day, think about the events of the day, putting more attention on the things you did well rather than on the little mistakes that you might have made. While relaxing in bed say to yourself something like: "This is the end of a wonderful day, I really liked the way I ...." Congratulate yourself for the good things that you did during the day - don't curse yourself for the little mistakes. In this way you will get to feel happy with who you are and, in turn, all your interactions will improve.

PROGRAMMING DURING SLEEP

We spend approximately one third of our lives asleep, but surprisingly no one really knows why we engage in this mysterious activity. It is not to rest our body, because switching off our consciousness is not essential to rest our physical body, and it is not to rest our brain, because although the frequency of brain waves decreases our brain is in many ways just as active while we are asleep. So, why do we sleep? The most promising theories propose that we sleep either: (a) to process and file information that was taken in during the day or (b) to dream.

It might be that we sleep to rest our consciousness or soul - a psychologist wouldn't agree with this though since, even though psychology is defined as "the study of the soul", most psychologists don't believe that we have one. The truth is that nobody really knows for sure why we sleep, but what is clear is that it is an essential activity and without it we would go mad within a very short time.

We can make good use of our sleeping time if we adjust our minds in a certain way just before going to sleep. One very useful practice is to train ourselves to remember our dreams, which is much easier than most people think and is useful for two reasons:

1)   The relaxation technique previously described, enables us to take information from the mind to the subconscious but not vice versa. Through our dreams we can establish a link which enables us to extract information lying within the subconscious.

2)   By carefully observing our dreams we can learn an enormous amount about ourselves. We can begin to discover aspects of our being which we were unaware of. This self-knowledge enables us to have more control over our lives.

Just by making the conscious decision that we want to remember our dreams, starts to create the changes within us that make it happen. Get into the habit of keeping a pen and paper by your bed and as soon as you wake up jot down a few lines about what you remember of your dreams. If you do this you will find that within a few weeks you will begin to remember more and more details about your dreams. This activity establishes a link between your mind and subconscious, and when that link is established it works both ways, carrying information both to and from your subconscious.

After just a few weeks of adjusting your mind to remember your dreams, they can give you information about yourself that you weren't consciously aware of, and you can programme them to answer certain questions about your life. The way to do this is to repeat to yourself over and over again a clear definite question while going to sleep, then the question will be programmed into your subconscious. For example, let's suppose you have a health problem. If you are ill, you can be sure that your body "knows" what is wrong and that there is a message for you somewhere in the illness. However, most of us are out of tune with our bodies and don't know how to listen to the messages that it gives us, and so we must learn how to listen. One way that this can be achieved is by relaxing deeply in a quiet environment and using our intuition to "feel" what the problem is. But this needs practice and an alternative method is to ask ourselves what the problem is just before we go to sleep. The answer may then come to us in our dreams either in an obvious way which could be immediately revealing or in symbolic form which we may need to analyse. It might be helpful to talk the dream through with someone but don't unquestioningly accept the interpretations of the so-called experts. Self-analysis of your dream, if it is done properly, is the most accurate and reliable way to discover its significance since only you know for sure what the contents of your dreams really mean. There are various ways to carry out this self-analysis. One way to do this is to sit down with a pen and paper and write down the heading "THE MEANING OF MY DREAM", then just start writing anything you can remember of the dream and whatever "spontaneously" comes into your consciousness. It is these spontaneous thoughts that often hold a great deal of wisdom. Another way to analyse your dream could be to have a good chat about it with a person who you can talk freely and openly with. The answer is then very likely to reveal itself in the course of the conversation. Try to maintain with confidence, a self-image of yourself as a person who has the answers to all the most important questions in your life. Dream interpretation is a big subject on which many, many books have been written. What I have related here only grazes the surface and if you are interested in going into any more detail, it may be worth consulting one or two of the numerous books available on the subject.

WHAT IS HYPNOSIS?

The phenomenon of hypnosis is shrouded in mystery and is highly misunderstood by the general public. The film industry is responsible for propagating much nonsense about hypnosis, and due to the stupid portrayal by this medium many people have totally the wrong idea of what it is. There are many people who don't even believe the phenomenon exists because the only "information" that they have about hypnosis is through watching some silly film on television.

Hypnosis, is basically the same phenomenon as self-suggestion, in that it is simply the penetration of commands into the subconscious while we are in a very relaxed state. **Hypnosis is simply a state of very deep relaxation at which time suggestions can be made.** The word is derived from the Greek word hypnos (υπνος) which means sleep.

In the eighteenth century, an Austrian doctor, Franz Anton Mesmer, thought he had discovered a cure for many diseases based on the theory of "animal magnetism". He performed complicated rituals with magnets and other objects in which he convinced people that they were going to be healed of their illnesses - and very often they were! The name of Mesmer is still a part of our vocabulary today when we speak of being "mesmerised" by something.

He was immensely successful due to his ability to implant suggestions in the minds of his patients by using a combination of methods. He probably didn't realise it, but his healing power was due to his very charismatic and persuasive character which enabled him to implant suggestions into the subconscious of his patients - this is the essence of the hypnotic technique. Due to his ability to convince people that they were going to get well they did! But neither he, nor his patients were aware that this is what was going on - everyone genuinely thought that it was the magnets that were causing the healing.

Unfortunately, when a commission was appointed to investigate into the validity of his theory and methods they concluded that "animal magnetism stemmed entirely from imagination" and so he was branded a fraud. This put the brakes on the development of the techniques that he used for nearly a hundred years, and even today there are still some doctors who see hypnotic techniques as either fraudulent or unethical. This is a great shame, since, if at that time the commission were appointed to test *the success rate* of mesmer's methods the outcome would have been very different, since, *he was* successful, even though the healing may have been occurring through a different process to what he thought. If, at that time, the commission were appointed for this objective, then it is possible that hypnosis would, by now, be a part of the education and training of every doctor, dentist and surgeon.

As long ago as 1892 the British Medical Association concluded that hypnosis *does* have very real therapeutic effects and can help to alleviate pain and induce sleep. Despite this it has taken another century for the technique to be taken seriously, it is only now beginning to be widely used as a complement to orthodox medical treatment.

The hypnotic trance is nothing mystical or strange but is just another state of consciousness. In fact, many hypnotists would say that it is not an altered state of consciousness, it is simply a state of highly focused attention. In fact, some hypnotists say that the hypnotic trance is not greatly different to intense concentration.

It is important to realise that everyone has a natural ability to go into a trance state and you have probably been in a trance-like state many times while just relaxing and staring into thin air. The reason that you may not have been aware that this was a hypnotic trance state is because you weren't subjected to any "strange" suggestions at that time.

Anyone can be hypnotised if they believe that they can and are willing to just go along with what the hypnotist says. However, no-one can be hypnotised if they believe that they can't and resist everything that they are told. If a hypnotist says something to you, it is what you tell yourself after that is important. So, if, for example, he says "you are feeling sleepy, your eyes are getting heavy" you can simply say to yourself "No they're not, I feel the same as always". However, if you decide to just relax and go along with what is said and not resist, then you will, *due to your own imagination,* find your eyes getting heavy and closing.

True hypnosis has nothing to do with gaining control over a hypnotic subject, on the contrary, it is about empowering someone so that they have more control over their life.

There is only one type of hypnosis -
self-hypnosis.

Whether we can be hypnotised or not depends as much on what we believe as on the skills of the hypnotist. If someone *believes* that a hypnotist could make them do anything, then the hypnotic subject is, by holding to this belief, voluntarily giving away all their own power and self-control and therefore could be influenced to behave in ways that might be out of character for them, similar perhaps to when they are drunk, but, they still wouldn't do anything that is against their moral code. For example, if someone is a peaceful, loving person and under hypnosis they are told to kill someone or commit any act that they would normally consider immoral, then they couldn't and wouldn't do it. This is one of the silliest misconceptions created by the film industry, where someone is told to commit murder and forget everything afterwards - it's sheer nonsense!

It is totally untrue that only weak-minded people can be hypnotised, anyone who can be suggested to - that is form a belief from what they hear - has the potential to be hypnotised. However, no-one can be hypnotised against their will *if they believe they can't.*

Real-life hypnosis is about your own control of yourself, your mind and body, and not at all about coming under the control of another person.
HELLMUT W. A. KARLE.

THE POWER OF HYPNOSIS

Since the contents of our imagination affects our mood and our emotional state, a hypnotist can change the way we are feeling just by simply asking us to imagine something - there is nothing amazing about this - we can do the same ourselves at any time simply by using our imagination to create vivid images.

If hypnosis is used sensibly and responsibly it is almost impossible to have any harmful effects. However, if the hypnotist is malicious and implants negative suggestions such as: "When you wake up you will feel really depressed and want to end your life", this could have undesirable consequences. However, as I said above, *it is what you tell yourself* that is the most important. For example, if a hypnotist tries to implant a nasty suggestion like this, you can simply say to yourself "No, when I wake up, I'm going to feel great" - then, when you wake up, you *will* feel great! Stage hypnosis, can sometimes be dangerous, if the hypnotist doesn't have concern for the well-being of the subject, which can often happen, since his aim is usually just to entertain and the subjects can then be left in a confused state, which can lead to harmful consequences.

The subconscious is not logical, it doesn't reason in the same way as the mind does. For example, if under hypnosis someone is told: "When I count to three your right foot will be stuck to the floor", the subconscious will not reason: "How is that possible without any glue or magnets?" It will get stuck, even if you are consciously thinking: "How can this be happening?" Similarly, it is possible, by getting appropriate suggestions into the subconscious, for your nose to itch every time you pick up a book; to start sneezing every time you eat a banana; to go red every time someone talks to you; to get a sore throat whenever your feet get slightly cold, or to yawn whenever you see someone yawn. All these conditions can be caused by suggestions programmed into your subconscious.

It is truly incredible what the body is capable of when the subconscious is appropriately programmed. For example, under hypnosis the body can become as limp as a rag or as stiff as a board; It can become resistant to the cold, to pain or discomfort, or even be oblivious to loud noises. If the hypnotist implants appropriate suggestions then within seconds someone can get a sore throat and start coughing, feel freezing cold or break out in a hot fever; they could eat their least favourite food as if they love it, or vice versa. Hypnosis has even been used in military situations to enable soldiers to resist giving away secrets during torture by increasing their tolerance to pain. Even more incredibly, operations have been carried out with hypnosis being used instead of anaesthetic - this is called hypnoanaesthesia and is safer than chemical anaesthesia since it can boost the immune system rather than repress it and reduce bleeding if suggestions are planted to this effect. So, If someone is hypnotised and told that during an operation their body will bleed very little then this will be the case. In other words, the subconscious is even capable of controlling the rate at which the body bleeds as well as reducing or eliminating pain - truly incredible!

If under hypnosis, a good hypnotic subject is told that they are going to be burned with a red hot poker, but instead are touched with a cold piece of metal, they will not only feel the pain as if the metal was hot, but more incredibly a blister can form even though there was no heat to cause the blister.

If you have a vivid imagination, try the following exercise which proves that you do have control over "involuntary" bodily processes. Hold a thermometer in your hand for a minute or so, and note down the temperature reading. Now, just *imagine* plunging your hand into freezing cold water, feel the lumps of ice knocking against your hand as you stir your hand in the icy water. Hold this image vividly for a couple of minutes and then note the temperature of the thermometer, it could be as much as two degrees colder than before, which shows that you do, after all, have control over your body temperature.

The implications of all this are astounding and we are led to the conclusion that our imagination and the suggestions planted in our subconscious affect our health in many ways. Below I have listed a few of these:

1) **Body temperature.** Suggestions programmed into the subconscious can determine our tolerance to the cold, how well we can resist the cold, and even how easily we sweat and shiver.

2) **Metabolic rate.** This may have an influence on our appetite, how easily we put on, or lose weight, and the general health of all our internal organs which are undergoing metabolic processes.

3) **Blood pressure and heart rate.** These factors determine the state of the heart.

4) **Production of antibodies.** This affects directly, how easily we get ill or recover from an illness.

5) **Digestive processes.** Depending on the type of suggestions, we could suffer from irritable bowel syndrome, constipation, diarrhoea, stomach ulcers, vomiting or psychosomatic food allergies and intolerances

6) **Hormone secretion.** Via the endocrine system, the subconscious can influence processes that we usually consider far from voluntary, such as our height, our weight, speed of healing, menstrual and reproductive processes, hair growth, and even breast size. The use of hypnosis for breast enlargement was discovered in 1969, and is based on the valid theory that the subconscious works on the autonomic nervous system which, in turn, controls the secretion of growth hormones secreted by the endocrine glands.

It is claimed that hypnosis, and, of course, the technique of self-suggestion, can help with all of the following conditions:

Addictions, alcoholism, anorexia, anxiety, asthma, back pain, bed-wetting, blushing, breast enlargement, bruxism, bulimia, cancer, diabetes, eczema, exam nerves, grief, hair growth problems, heart problems, high blood-pressure, incontinence, inferiority complex, insomnia, intestinal problems, irritable bowel, lethargy, low concentration, low blood pressure, migraine, nail biting, nervous diarrhoea, obsessions, pain, peptic ulcers, phobias, sexual problems, smoking, sterility, stomach problems, stress, stuttering, tension, thumb sucking, tinnitus, and weight problems.

If you are sceptical of these claims, this is fine if it is doubt with openness, but don't allow your scepticism to close your mind to possibilities. The mind and the subconscious have a much more powerful effect than many people realise - what is within us, is far more important, in all respects, to our state of health and well-being than what is happening outside us. If you accept the incredible potential that you can release from within you if you are able to reprogramme your subconscious by practising the technique of self-suggestion, your life will change for the better, in ways that you never imagined possible.

Example
Suggestions

Example Suggestions

I have included these example suggestions here as a guide to some of the possible applications of the technique of self-suggestion. This part of the book is to be used differently to the rest of the book. Don't simply read through the examples, in the same way as you would read any text. Try something like the following:

Take this book out with you when you go for a walk, and as you walk read number 1, think about it for a few seconds, feel it, decide if it would be useful to believe it to be totally true for you. If so, tick it, and come back to it later as a suggestion that you can use during your relaxation sessions. Read number 2 carefully, and repeat as above.

Whenever you come across a sentence for which you think "that doesn't apply to me, I wish I were ...., but I'm not", then this may be what you need to work on even more. For example, if you read: "I am a confident, successful person", and you think: "but I'm not!", then give this a double tick.

If you read one after the other and think to yourself: "I wish that were true......", you may come to realise how you have been self-sabotaging yourself with your thoughts up to now.

It is a very useful exercise to make up your own suggestions, but if you don't, the selection below contains various suggestions for a whole range of effects from becoming more confident to curing illnesses.

1)   I am now creating the wonderful reality that I desire.

2) I now have control over my subconscious and can achieve anything that I want to achieve in life.

3) I am a very positive person. I always focus on the positive aspects of any situation.

4) I always sit, stand and walk with a good deportment.

5) I am a happy, contented person.

6) I am a very confident, successful person.

7) I am a very easy-going person.

8) I look at all my challenges with a smile and realise that every problem has a solution - even if it is through acceptance.

9) My mind works clearly and I find it extremely easy to learn.

10) I have a very retentive memory.

11) I have excellent concentration.

12) I have the wisdom within me to answer any questions that I may have about myself or about life.

13) I am in touch with my inner voice and have excellent intuition.

14) I have enormous energy and vitality.

15) My positive outlook releases energy within me which enables me to do anything that I want to do in life.

16) My body is in harmony with my mind.

17) My immune system is strong. I have an excellent resistance to illness.

18) My heart is strong and my circulation is good.

19) My digestion is good and I have a regular bowel movement every day.

20) My digestive system is so healthy that it can convert toxins into harmless chemicals.

21) I eat only that which I know is good for me.

22) I love fresh fruit and salads. Sweet, processed foods are totally unappealing to me.

23) I am a peaceful, loving, compassionate human being.

24) I am a warm, loving, friendly person and I am spiritually open in all my interactions with people.

25) I always finish any job that I start, unless it is inappropriate to do so.

26) I am a creative, original person.

27) I am a strong, courageous person.

28) I am an honest person and I always tell the truth.

29) I have integrity and I only do what I know is right

30) I love myself and feel happy about being me.

31) I enjoy going out in all weathers. I love to be in touch with the elements.

32) I love the cold, and enjoy the feeling of a wintry breeze blowing against my face.

33) I feel totally comfortable with my sexuality. I love my body, it is a wonderful expression of life.

34) Sexual feelings are normal and natural. I can freely receive pleasure from my body.

35) I freely forgive all who have hurt me in my life.

36) I sleep really well at night. I always wake up at the right time feeling wonderfully refreshed.

37) I see immense beauty in all of nature

38) I feel a deep sense of inner peace.

39) I love life and feel in harmony with the universe.

40) I find it easy to do the things that are necessary to make the desired changes in my life.

Remember that
this moment is
the first moment
of the rest of your life.
It is the thoughts that
you choose to occupy your mind
with from this moment on
that will create or
influence the
rest of your life.

Suggestions To Change Your Life

Suggestions to change your life

You can use the technique of self-suggestion to work on many aspects of your life. You can use it to improve your memory and concentration, help you to learn more easily, help you to make decisions, lose weight, eat healthier foods, stop smoking, improve your health, enhance your sex life, exercise more, resist the cold, increase your self-esteem, develop your intuition, become more sensitive and loving, or to treat any of the conditions listed at the end of the section on *The power of hypnosis.*

This final chapter focuses on some of the most common areas that individuals may wish to work on. You can, if you wish, use this section in the manner of a reference text - reading and focusing on those sections which are of specific interest to you.

Many people would be able to accept the idea that by using the technique of self-suggestion, you could change your mood or even overcome illness, but they would probably think it impossible to change characteristics that they have always considered innate. So, I will start with one such example of which I have personal experience - intelligence. I am defining intelligence here as the ability to absorb information in an efficient way and to think clearly and make connections between the various aspects of knowledge that you have. This is often considered to be an innate, unchangeable quality of a human being - you are either intelligent or you are not! But is this the case? I believe not.

ENHANCE YOUR LEARNING ABILITY

The first time that I faithfully used the technique of self-suggestion was during my first year at university while I was an undergraduate student studying physics and mathematics. I was having a little trouble understanding some of the mathematics - there was an enormous amount of information being thrown at us and I was beginning to feel a bit bogged-down with all the work. So, every night as I relaxed in bed before going to sleep I told myself things like: "I love mathematics, I find it really easy" and "I really enjoy learning and my mind is working very clearly to absorb, comprehend and learn these fascinating concepts." Also, as I woke up in the morning I spent about half an hour deeply relaxing and suggesting to myself: "I am really looking forward to going to college today, I will easily learn everything that I need to learn" and "I have good concentration, a good memory and my mind works clearly". Also, and most importantly, I visualised myself in the class smiling, feeling good, enjoying the lesson, understanding everything and finding the subject easy. I was amazed at the change that occurred in me in a very short time. Within a few days I started to feel more relaxed about the work. I was enjoying it and understanding it more, and I felt the overall learning process was much more efficient.

I am now convinced that **when students have great difficulty in learning something, it is mainly because of "mental blocks" that have arisen due to a negative self-image about their ability to learn.** This could have been caused by repeatedly being called stupid when they were younger, or the mental blocks could have been programmed in by bad teaching which caused discouragement and frustration, or by being ridiculed when they didn't understand something, or it could have been caused by telling themselves over a period of time "I hate this subject".

If it is true that a person's learning ability and clarity of thought is determined by mental blocks, produced by a negative self-image, and I believe it is, it means that if someone can remove these mental blocks then *they can actually become more intelligent*, since, as I said before, intelligence is a measure of how easily someone absorbs information and how clearly they think. Even though many people may not want a formal education, *everyone* wants to know how to get on in life. Using the technique of self-suggestion you can develop your ability to learn and improve your intelligence, your powers of concentration, and your memory.

It is very encouraging to realise that so-called "innate characteristics" *are* changeable, since they are generally dependent on changeable factors such as self-image, self-esteem, self-love, and self-confidence.

IMPROVE YOUR DIET

Self-suggestion can be used for slimming, if someone is overweight due to lack of exercise, or not being able to resist sweet, high-calorie foods. Surprisingly, it is also effective, with a bit more work, for someone who doesn't over-eat or under-eat but has weight problems due to hormonal imbalances which produce a very slow or fast metabolic rate. Hormone production *can be* adjusted by subconscious programming since the endocrine system is governed by the autonomic nervous system, which in turn, receives it's instructions from the subconscious. If someone has disturbed the natural hormone balance by negative suggestions implanted into the subconscious, a considerable amount of work is needed to change this programming. Self-suggestion, if used earnestly, may be sufficient, but for severe eating disorders I would recommend getting the help of a professional hypnotherapist.

It is essential to realise at the outset that every human being has a very strong, innate, subconscious urge to eat when hungry, and therefore no suggestion should try to overcome this natural urge.

For example, it is not at all sensible to make suggestions such as "I don't get hungry anymore" or "when I get hungry I am no longer tempted to eat" because this is going against our basic nature. Although, it is probably true to say that it is not impossible, with enough negative suggestions regarding food, to actually dislike food so much that we never want to eat, but this surely must be the worst way that anyone could diet.

You can eat as much fruit and vegetables as you want, within reason, and so, whether you are on a diet or whether you want to limit your diet to so-called healthy foods, the most important factor is to adjust your subconscious programming regarding what you want to eat rather than how much. If you have a choice between a bar of chocolate or an apple, what do you usually choose?

Every human being is tempted towards that which will give them pleasure or *what they have been conditioned to believe* will give them pleasure. For example, if a child is always given cakes and sweets as a treat or as a reward for good behaviour, but is "forced" to eat fruit, then the result may be that they will grow up into an adult who doesn't particularly like fruit but loves "to treat themself" to the occasional chocolate bar or whatever. Maybe if children were forced to eat sweets, or at least not given them as a reward, then they might lose much of their appeal. When people are brought up with this conditioning, associating sweets with reward they feel a temptation to eat these products not only because of the physiological addiction to the sweetness, but also due to their subconscious programming. If this is your situation, and if you see it as a problem, then using self-suggestion and visualisation you can begin to change the way that you look at sweets. The worst thing that you can do if you are trying to resist certain foods is to tell yourself "I just can't resist it!" or imagine those cakes and sweets as delicious and irresistible.

A VISUALISATION EXERCISE:

Here is an excellent technique for increasing the appeal of fruit and decreasing the appeal of sweets: While you are sitting relaxed, close your eyes and form an image in your mind of a large, beautiful, juicy, apple (or any other fruit), hold the image in full colour, now imagine picking it up and biting into it - it tastes absolutely delicious. While doing this, repeat the suggestion: "I love fresh fruit, it is delicious and is really good for me". Now, in your mind put down the fruit and imagine a slice of cake in front of you (or any other sweet that you want to resist). It is a small image and it looks very boring and unappealing, hold the image in black and white, now imagine yourself biting into the cake and feeling repulsed by it - it tastes disgustingly sweet. (This is one of the few situations where imagining the negative is effective!) Now repeat the suggestion: "I find unhealthy, sickly foods such as sweets and cakes disgusting". If you do this little exercise for 5 minutes every day for a week, you will find yourself going for the apple rather than the cake without any effort at all.

If you have a weight problem then during the relaxation sessions you should try visualisation exercises as well as self-suggestion. While deeply relaxed you can visualise yourself with the perfect body (whatever you think that is!) and see yourself eating and enjoying the foods that you consider healthy such as high protein or low fat foods, fresh fruit or salads. Imagine yourself smiling while walking, running, swimming or whatever. Then tell yourself something like: "I love eating healthy foods such as fresh fruit and salads" and "I feel good about my beautiful body". If you feel some resistance to this latter suggestion, then it is probably one which is particularly valuable for you to repeat as often as possible.

Because our image-conscious society puts an unhealthy emphasis on looking a certain way, it has created obsessions about slimming which often gives rise to a type of dieting which isn't healthy. There is now considerable evidence to suggest that inconsistent dieting is not good for the health, because the body adapts to whatever type of food it receives, and so the body needs a while to readjust whenever the dietary intake changes. What the body requires is consistency and so the worst way to diet is to go through large changes frequently - sometimes over indulging, other times fasting, one week fruit diets, the next week the hay diet, and so on. It is *much better* not to diet at all, than to diet for a week or two and then go back to "normal". However, fasting for one day a week on a permanent basis, drinking only water and fruit juice on that day, has been shown to be beneficial to the health.

Be careful not to become too obsessed about physical appearance or size. Unfortunately, the media conditions us to believe that facial features and figure are the most important factors in becoming an attractive person. They are not. Although, as human beings we have a strong attraction towards what we are conditioned to see as beauty, we have an even stronger and more instinctive magnetism towards a person's inner qualities that inevitably win people's hearts. As you develop from within, you will become more attractive, even if your physical features don't change. But, in fact, to a certain extent some of your physical features will change, since what shows on the outside is an expression of what lies on the inside. So, as you become more spiritual, self-confident and happy within yourself, this will show in every gesture, movement, smile, posture and tone of voice. In this way, people will inevitably find you more attractive. You will begin to radiate a certain energy which, although people might not be consciously aware of, they can't help being attracted to.

Many so-called weight problems are not really weight problems at all, they are self-esteem problems. Very often if someone works on developing their self-esteem then their "weight problems" will automatically disappear. So, unless you really do have such a severe weight problem that it is threatening your health, I recommend using suggestions which make you feel happy about your body, and just eat sensibly and enjoy your food - in this way most eating disorders automatically disappear and the body stabilises to a *healthy* weight.

The healthiest way to diet is to be *consistent,* eating a balanced diet of natural, unprocessed, fresh foods which contain a good balance of protein, carbohydrate, fat, vitamins and minerals. However, having said that, there is a very important principle from Ayurvedic medicine that **a healthy digestive system can turn poisons into nectar, but an unhealthy digestive system can turn nectar into poison.** We can learn an enormous amount from the ancient wisdom of the east, particularly Ayurvedic medicine and traditional Chinese medicine - these sciences contain models of the human being which are more holistic than western orthodox medicine. One useful teaching from ayurveda is:

> *You are not what you eat,*
> *you are what you do with what you eat.*
> *AYURVEDIC PRINCIPLE.*

So, it is important to try not to be obsessive about what you eat, since this could have an effect on the digestive system. If you put a bias towards fresh, wholesome, natural foods, and you sometimes eat so-called "unhealthy" foods, don't waste time worrying about possible harmful effects - they are probably non-existent, and if there are any harmful effects from what you eat, there is a strong possibility that the worry was a contributory factor.

STOP SMOKING

This section is written for those who feel that they are addicted to the smoking habit but have the desire to give up. Many people find it very difficult to give up smoking, not only because of the physical addiction, but because *they see themselves as a smoker who just can't give up*. First of all you must realise that if several million people have given up smoking then *obviously* you can too. What you need to do is prepare yourself a few weeks in advance by telling yourself continuously "The next time I attempt to give up smoking I am going to achieve it with ease". Tell yourself this for a few weeks - when you wake up, while going to sleep, while walking along the street, or at any odd moment in the day. You must also convince yourself that if you stop smoking your life will be better in every way.

Next, set yourself a date to give up, say, 4 weeks after you start the preliminary suggestions. Tell everyone you know that from that date you will no longer be a smoker, this has a very definite effect of increasing your commitment to keep to it. During those few weeks think about what a horrible habit smoking is and how much you want to give up and thankfully how easy you are going to find it to do so. Spend about 20 minutes every day in relaxation telling yourself many negative things about smoking such as: "Smoking is such a stupid, mindless thing to do - I find it easy to stop this ridiculous habit".

Because we are creatures of habit, it might be necessary, initially, to also give up certain activities that you associate with smoking, for example if you always have a cup of coffee and a cigarette at eleven o'clock you might also need to give up the coffee at this time, for a while. Within a fairly short time, once you no longer have any temptation to smoke, you can resume your coffee if you wish.

In the case of making any change to your life, it is always better to motivate yourself by focusing on what you are trying to move towards, rather than what you are trying to move away from, although sometimes motivation can be strongest when both factors are present. For example, in the case of trying to give up smoking, in addition to considering your improved health and money savings, you could also focus on the disgusting smell produced by stale tobacco and the cough in the morning.

About 2 weeks before the date set for giving up, have a 15 minute session of relaxation everyday, or at least, once every two days, including verbal suggestions and visualisations on the disgusting aspects of smoking and the wonderful aspects of giving up. On the planned date, set aside at least half an hour to relax, because when you finish that relaxation session you are going to be an ex-smoker. During the relaxation session picture yourself as an ex-smoker who finds it really easy to resist. Imagine the unpleasant aspects of smoking such as smelly clothes and disgusting full ash-trays. Imagine yourself inhaling the smoke from a cigarette while looking really stupid - think about how ridiculous you appear inhaling poisonous gases. It can also be very effective if, while you are in a relaxed state, you consider the worst possible consequences of continuing to smoke - disease, death, your loved ones grieving for you, and so on. Visualise this image as clearly as you can, so that it gives you an unpleasant feeling which you would rather not have. Hold this image for as long as possible until the feeling reaches its peak and then out loud or internally shout "NO". Smoking is now a thing of the past. Think about all the advantages - being able to taste and smell food better, a large saving in money, no cough in the morning and fresh clothes. While holding the self-image of a non-smoker repeat to yourself a suggestion which conveys to you in the positive that you are now never going to smoke another cigarette, and that you are a non-smoker. For example you could repeat "I am free", or "I am clean". Repeat this sentence of your choice to yourself over and over again, between 10 and 100 times. If you wish you could shorten it to "I am a non-smoker", or you could use any other sentence which would convey this important message to your subconscious.

If you are a very heavy smoker (50-80 a day), then I would first advise cutting down, before stopping altogether, this is because the physical addiction can be very powerful, and so stopping suddenly can be a shock to the system. You can use self-suggestion to help with this as well, for example, if you smoke 50 a day, first cut down to 20 a day for a few months using a suggestion such as: "I now only smoke 20 a day and that is more than enough"; then, after smoking just 20 a day, or less, for a while, you will be ready to stop altogether using the method described above. You will find that - if you expect success - within a short time you will achieve it.

OVERCOME SEXUAL PROBLEMS

Sexual desire is an innate subconscious urge, which means that it was pre-programmed before birth. However, sexual activity, sexual inhibitions, and intensity of pleasure received from sex, all depend on what you have learned and on what has been programmed into your subconscious during the course of your life. These suggestions determine how you feel about sex and your sexuality, the kind of sexual activity that appeals to you, how much you enjoy it and even to a certain extent how often you desire it.

There are several different types of sexual problems, but I will only discuss here the two most common types of problem. The most important thing to realise about sexual problems is that the vast majority have a psychological origin. The two main categories are.

1)   Performance problems - usually created by worrying about not being able to satisfy your partner.
2)   Inhibition problems - not being able to give or receive sexual pleasure due to negative social or religious conditioning regarding sex.

I will deal with each of these in turn.

PERFORMANCE PROBLEMS

The main cause of sexual problems for the sexually inexperienced, comes from worry and anxiety about how successful they will be in satisfying their partner - this is known as "performance anxiety". The statement *what you expect will become your reality,* is especially true in sexual situations. So, if someone worries about how well they will "perform" in bed, the worry can certainly have a detrimental effect on what happens. The result of performance anxiety is usually to create the very condition that you are worried about. The most common symptoms are impotence, premature ejaculation and vaginismus.

If a woman worries that she may be boring or unable to satisfy her partner in a sexual situation, then she is more likely to be unrelaxed and therefore more inhibited and tense, which will inevitably lead to the result that she dreaded. The same is true for a man, if he worries that he may not "perform" very well then the worry will certainly cause inhibiting effects. In addition, if he worries that he may not achieve or maintain a satisfactory erection or suffer from premature ejaculation, then the dread can bring about these unfortunate conditions, and if it happens once, then the worry, fear and anxiety may have the effect of worsening the condition.

An ongoing sexual problem of this type within a relationship, could have first occurred due to any number of reasons, such as, feeling worried or anxious about your sexual performance, feeling stressed from too much work, being too tired at that particular moment, being unsure about the sexual partner that you were with, or any other reason which might have made you feel worried, anxious, tense or uncomfortable. It could have, potentially, been just a one-off occurrence but ended up as a sexual problem because of the self-perpetuating worry.

If you have a sexual problem that *seems to have* a physical origin that causes you worry, then for your peace of mind it might be a good idea to see a doctor so that you can be reassured that the problem isn't physical, which it almost certainly isn't. Once you realise that the problem isn't physical but is basically a self-created psychosomatic condition, you are more than half-way to overcoming it. A few steps that you may like to try to overcome any number of sexual problems are given at the end of this section.

INHIBITION PROBLEMS
An upbringing which associates sex with immorality does a considerable amount of harm, and a great deal of positive suggestion is required to counteract the negative effects of this conditioning. If someone is brought up being conditioned with absurd ideas such as: the genitals are dirty, you shouldn't touch yourself, masturbation is harmful, oral sex is unnatural, sexual aids are immoral, and so on, then they have little chance of having a fulfilling sexual relationship unless they can transcend these crazy ideas. Someone who has been conditioned to believe that sex is dirty or sinful may suffer from any number of problems, such as low libido, impotence, vaginismus, and, above all, sexual frustration.

To enjoy sex to the maximum you have got to feel okay about your sexuality and know that sexual feelings are totally normal. For couples who can talk freely and openly about sex as comfortably as they might talk about food, politics or any other topic, it is much more likely that they will have a full and satisfying sex life. If they have an unsatisfactory session one night, the most sensible attitude to take might be one of: "Oh well, it wasn't that good tonight, but it doesn't matter, I'm sure that it will be okay tomorrow." However, the likelihood of the unsatisfying session turning into a sexual problem increases for those who consider sex a taboo subject. What happens in this case between many couples is that the lack of clear communication creates thoughts such as: "oh no, I hope that doesn't happen again tomorrow" or "we now have a problem" (and once you think you have a problem then you have a problem).

Sometimes inhibition problems can be caused by one partner being less adventurous than the other might like. This could be due to strong negative religious or social conditioning regarding sex, and can lead to frustration and dissatisfaction in both partners.   In this situation it may be advisable to see a psychosexual counsellor or sex therapist.

MAXIMISING THE PLEASURE FROM SEX
How easily this can be achieved depends on the extent of any previous negative conditioning that you may have had regarding sex. If you had years of being taught that it is a sinful activity then it might require a considerable amount of work consisting of many repetitions of suggestions such as:
"I know how to really please my partner", or, "sex is a totally natural activity and I give myself full permission to enjoy it", or, "I always take the time to give my partner that they desire".

Here are a few extra pieces of advice, which can move you towards eliminating any sexual problems that you may have and helping you to receive the maximum pleasure from sex:

1)   Let go of any pre-conceived ideas of how it should be.

2)   Try to be as uninhibited and adventurous as possible.

3)   Give yourself full permission to enjoy it.

4)   Practice talking openly about sex.

5)   Express your fantasies to your partner.

6)   Consider using sex aids if required.

7)   Read some of the intelligently written books on the subject.

8)   Repeat positive suggestions regularly, to help you feel okay about sex and your sexuality.

9)   If you have any deep-seated, negative, social or religious conditioning about sex, consider seeing a psychosexual counsellor.

INCREASE YOUR TOLERANCE TO PAIN

He that is uneasy at every little pain
is never without some ache.
PROVERB.

Before carrying out any suggestions to diminish or eliminate pain we must be fully aware that pain is present for a reason - if it is from an injury it might be saying "be careful", or if it is from an apparently self-created ailment, it may be present to teach us something very important about our life-style, posture, diet, or whatever. If we can listen carefully to the message that the pain is trying to convey, then we may be able to get rid of it, in a very simple way without any medical intervention whatsoever. To take a simple analogy - if someone came to you with tragic news, would you kill the messenger so that the tragedy no longer exists?

This is very similar to what is happening when someone takes a pain killer to eliminate a pain which might be present for a very good reason. When we consider the fact that pain may be trying to convey an important message to us, or warn us about something, then ignoring it, or struggling to get rid of it, is as foolish as disconnecting the oil warning light from a car, when it is flashing, instead of simply adding oil to the engine.

> *The body is our primary feedback mechanism*
> *that can show us what is and isn't working about our*
> *ways of thinking, expressing and living.*
> *SHAKTI GAWAIN.*

It is possible, using self-suggestion while in a trance state, to create total numbness in a certain body part, or to free ourselves from pain when it is present. It is also possible to increase our tolerance to pain in any situation so that the same pain has a much smaller effect. Pain coping suggestions can be very useful for women during pregnancy and labour. Most women, (but not all), suffer considerable pain during childbirth, which can often be made worse by tension, fear and worry.

> *Sometimes we suffer,*
> *not from the pain itself, but from*
> *the resistance to the pain.*

Self-healing can be very powerfully initiated by the very simple process of taking your awareness into the body part that requires healing. The healing power of your awareness can be enhanced by feeling positive feelings towards your own body. The process of directing your attention into your foot, for example, sends an energy which begins healing immediately. If a part of your body is causing you pain, do you curse it or bless it? It is an important aspect of self-healing to be able to send loving energy to the ailing part - similar theory applies as with a naughty child - sending energy through love has an infinitely greater chance of improving any condition or situation than sending energy through anger and resentment. It may sound like a strange bit of advice to focus love on a painful part of your anatomy but there are countless examples where this has created healing.

If we consider the factors that determine our pain threshold in situations of rough sports or in the dentist's chair, a very important factor is self-image. If someone has a self-image of being very fragile due to always telling themselves: "I haven't got a very good tolerance to pain" or "I just can't take any pain" then they will find it very difficult to cope with pain when it arises. But if someone has the opposite self-image and tells themselves: "There's nothing wrong with a bit of pain, I'm tough" then they will be able to deal with a lot more pain. So, if you want to increase your tolerance to pain, try any of the following suggestions, or make up your own:

1)   I am really tough, I have enormous resistance to pain.

2)   I find it really easy to ignore pain now, it doesn't bother me at all anymore.

3)   I am looking forward to the next time I go to the dentist because it is a wonderful challenge to my inner strength.

4)   When I am in a dentist's chair, the sound of the drill makes me feel comfortable and relaxed.

RESIST THE COLD

Very few people would go and see a therapist because they feel cold - they simply put on a jumper! But feeling the cold is something that affects the quality of life of many people and since it is under subconscious control it can be adjusted by self-suggestion. Every individual has a similar *potential* ability to deal with the cold, but their actual ability depends on their subconscious programming. Two people could have similar bodies, with equal layers of fat, hair and muscle, but they could feel the cold very differently depending on what lies in the subconscious, and on their attitude to the cold.

How we feel about the cold or about the weather generally, is greatly affected by hearing many, many times during our childhood comments such as: "Oh no, it's raining", "Isn't it a miserable day", "It's very cold out and you can get ill if you get cold", "It's too hot to go out today", "It's too windy", "Wrap up well or you'll catch your death of cold", and so on. All these **negative suggestions can have the effect of distancing you from nature and making you feel less happy about being alive.** If you had years of being told: "Wrap up well or you'll catch your death of cold", you may have to work hard to change your subconscious programming and adapt your body, but it will be well worthwhile - imagine being able to wait for a bus in winter with an icy breeze blowing and a smile on your face while enjoying the fresh feeling of the air on your face. Remember that **the result of any situation depends on your attitude to it.**

When I was a child I remember often sitting in bed comfortably reading, and then one day while I was relaxing, my grandmother came in and said to me with conviction: "Cover your shoulders or they will get cold". I was about 10 years old and like any child of this age I ignored my grandmother's "good advice" which she repeated several times. However, within a very short time my shoulders started to feel cold and then *I had to* cover them. For several years after, I suffered from cold shoulders while sitting up in bed reading until I came to the awareness that this condition was caused by the subconscious rather than by the cold. I had been "hypnotised" by my grandmother's comments and suffered the consequences for many years. She told me in a very definite way "your shoulders *will* get cold", and my subconscious took it literally, even though I didn't consciously believe it. But, in time I learned how to overcome "the hypnotic spell" that I was under - I formed various positive suggestions such as "I feel really cosy and warm while I lie in bed reading" which I repeated to myself many times over several days until I no longer suffered from cold shoulders. Many people suffer all through life unnecessarily, by having taken on board destructive beliefs like this. I wonder how many over-protective parents or grandparents have caused illnesses by inadvertently putting negative suggestions into the subconscious of their loved ones. E.g. "If you walk on the kitchen floor with bare feet you will get ill." Have you ever been subjected to negative suggestions like this? It might be true to say that: "standing on a cold kitchen floor in winter *might* lower your resistance to illness", but then again it might not! Grandma would do much less harm if she made the suggestion like this rather than dogmatically stating that you *will* get ill.

What is your programming? Is it: "I hate the cold", "I really feel the cold", "The cold gives me a sore throat and makes me ill". Or is it: "The cold doesn't bother me", "I don't feel the cold", "I love the feeling of a cold breeze on my face, it is wonderfully refreshing". What you tell yourself when you go out makes an enormous difference to how your body responds. Some people can actually "fear" the cold due to years of being told: "You'll catch your death". It could then be this fear that create any harmful effects of the cold, and not the cold itself.

If you want to make a change in your life in this respect and develop a more positive attitude towards the cold, you must first acquire the belief that the cold is usually harmless. Cold does not cause illness unless your *internal body temperature* lowers for a sustained period of time. Most people who feel cold only have a lower skin temperature and this definitely *does not* cause illness. If you go for a brisk walk on a cold winter's day without a coat on, your *skin temperature* will lower but this will not make you ill since your internal body temperature is still constant at 37 °C. However, if you fall asleep on a park bench on a mild autumn day and your *internal body temperature* lowers, causing you to wake up shivering, there is much more chance of becoming ill - but it is still only a possibility and not a certainty, and will depend to a large extent on your attitude and your subconscious programming. If you do get ill whenever you feel the slightest bit cold, it's probably because you have a subconscious instruction that causes it. What do you expect will happen if, whenever you go out, you tell yourself: "Oh no, I feel cold, I'm going to get ill now"?

A few examples of suggestions to try are:
1)   I love the cold, it is invigorating and refreshing.
2)   I enjoy the feeling of a fresh breeze on my face in winter.
3)   I love all the variations of weather that nature offers. (See page 13).

It is important not to go too far in practising resisting the cold. For example, it would not be very sensible, if you are used to fur coats, to try walking out in the snow for an hour a day in your vest. I am recommending sensible clothing along with a sensible positive attitude towards the weather - and just enjoy it.

DEALING WITH FEARS AND PHOBIAS

If there's something to fear,
it's the feeling of fear on its own.
If there's something to dread,
it's the dread that the feeling has grown.
ANDREA PHOTIOU.

If you are in a certain situation and then for whatever reason you feel fear and start to panic, then a similar situation at any time in the future could cause the same panic reaction, reinforcing even more, the negative subconscious command. Highly emotional experiences can have an enormous effect on the subconscious to programme it to cause inappropriate or illogical behaviour in response to certain triggers.

I once knew a girl, who I will refer to here as Jane, who had a fear of tube trains - this fear is called metrophobia. For Jane, the fear began one day while she was travelling on an over-crowded tube and the train stopped in a tunnel for a little while. Her imagination started working over-time - she began to imagine becoming trapped and the possibility of a collision occurring. These thoughts caused Jane to feel very uncomfortable, she became very tense, started sweating, and showed other symptoms of a panic attack. This highly emotional experience programmed the subconscious to receive the command: tube = panic, which lead to the metrophobia which she subsequently suffered from. The next time that Jane went on a tube she suffered a panic attack because her subconscious was now programmed to panic when triggered by similar surroundings to those that were present during the initial panic attack. This occurrence reinforced the programming which caused the phobia to become even stronger, and, in fact, it got to the point where she would panic by just *thinking* about entering a tube. Jane eventually overcame her phobia by using the technique of self-suggestion coupled with the help of a good hypnotherapist.

Whatever the type of phobia, or whatever the cause, positive self-suggestions can help. The view presented here of the cause of phobias, is slightly over-simplified, since every phobia and every individual is different. Many phobias may begin in the way described above, but there is always an underlying cause, such as an extreme inferiority complex, low self-esteem or feelings of insecurity. For example, someone with an enormous inferiority complex may have agoraphobia because they are frightened to leave the house because of an intense feeling of not being able to cope with the situations that they may encounter.

A man who fears suffering
is already suffering from what he fears.
MICHEL DE MONTAIGNE.

ANOTHER METHOD OF REPROGRAMMING THE SUBCONSCIOUS

Just as highly emotional experiences can programme phobias into our subconscious, we can employ our emotions to release us from negative fears and emotions. It is possible to reprogramme yourself in a positive way by generating a lot of emotion while shouting and screaming positive suggestions with a lot of feeling. This may not be a suitable method for everyone, but for some it is more effective than the relaxation technique. It is interesting that, although what I am describing here seems to be the opposite to self-suggestion by deep relaxation, the result is the same - to reprogramme the subconscious.

I will describe the method in more detail using arachnaphobia as an example - this is a good technique for those who have such a fear of spiders that just the thought of one sends them into a state of panic, since, if this is the case, the relaxation method may be ineffective since it would be difficult for them to relax and to think about a spider at the same time.

CURING ARACHNAPHOBIA
Set aside about an hour or so when you can just be alone without any disturbance. Think about how your fear of spiders has adversely affected the quality of your life in many situations. Dwell on this. Go over situations in your mind of various times

when you felt fear. Get upset and worked up about it until you generate an intense desire to rid yourself of the fear. You may want to cry or hit a cushion. When you are feeling very emotionally charged, shout ENOUGH and then yell out, with emotion, whatever you desire in the positive. For example:

1)   Spiders are harmless little creatures.

2)   Spiders no longer have any effect on my well-being, they are totally insignificant to me now.

Shout whatever comes into your mind. As long as the intention is present to transcend the phobia and you say what you say with plenty of emotion then one session could be enough to eliminate the fear forever.

Although I have described this method for arachnaphobia, it can be used to cure any type of phobia, or even other negative emotional states such as extreme jealousy, resentment, hate or anger. For those who have deep emotional wounds, this technique could be more effective than the relaxation technique previously described.

HEAL YOUR EYES

How healthy our eyes are, depend on many factors, the two most important are, the type of exercise we give them, our general state of bodily health, dietary factors, and our subconscious programming related to their functioning. There is now considerable evidence to suggest that our subconscious programming does indeed affect our eyesight.

The subconscious may affect our eyes in various ways:
1)   How sensitive our eyes are to light.
2)   How our eyes feel when we wake up in the morning.

3)   How sensitive our eyes are to dust, smoke or onions.

4)   Our eyesight and vision - that is how well our eyes are able to focus on objects both near and far, and how well our brain interprets the information received from the eye.

Consider this question: "Does too much reading damage your eyes or is it *the belief* that too much reading can damage your eyes, that does the damage? I think that it may be a combination of both, but the belief plays the greater part, if it is held long enough to be programmed into the subconscious.

If a person were hypnotised and told: "when you wake up you will look at the picture on that wall, and, as you do so, your eyes will immediately go blurred and you will find it difficult to focus clearly" this would certainly affect their eye-sight to some extent at that time. It is very possible that bad eyesight may sometimes begin as a psychosomatic condition and then due to the wearing of contact lenses or spectacles a dependency on these corrective lenses results. In fact, there is now growing evidence to suggest that wearing glasses or contact lenses is the main *cause* of defective vision. There is a growing awareness that the eyes are just like any other part of our body which have their off days, and may sometimes feel tired or strained and may need a rest before they function perfectly again. If a person goes to an optician at a time like this they could be condemned to wearing glasses for the rest of their life simply because their eyes happened to be a bit tired at the time that they were tested. To make a simple analogy, if you had weak leg muscles, would you use crutches on a permanent basis? If you did, what do you think would happen to your legs? Some ophthalmologists claim that, if the eyes are looked after and exercised and given the correct nutrition, then glasses would, in most cases, be totally unnecessary.

Even if you wear corrective lenses, there are various eye exercises which can stop the deterioration of your eyesight, and, if combined with self-suggestion, it might be possible to restore perfect eyesight, so that glasses are no longer required. For more information read *Better sight without glasses* by Harry Benjamin, published by Thorsons, and *improve your vision without glasses or contact lenses* published by fireside books.

A few suggestions to try are:
1)   My vision is perfect.
2)   I have perfect eyesight.
3)   I can see comfortably and clearly.
4)   My eyes are healthy and strong.

SENSITIVITY TO LIGHT
If the reactions of a group of people sitting at a white barbecue table on a bright summers day is observed, it is interesting to see how differently everyone is affected by the sunlight reflected from the table. Some seem totally undisturbed while others can hardly open their eyes. It is possible that the people who can't stand bright light actually have eyes of a different nature which are inherently more sensitive, but I think that it is more likely that they are more sensitive to the light because *they believe* that they are, since they have programmed into their subconscious that "I can't stand bright light". The way that the eyes respond to light depends on what is programmed into the subconscious rather than on an inherent sensitivity.

A few years ago a friend of mine told me that he could only sleep if it was pitch dark, and that the slightest glimmer of light coming through the keyhole, or a gap under the door, would keep him awake. What was stopping him from getting to sleep was not the light itself but his self-image of being someone who can't get to sleep if there is any light present

If someone can't sleep when there is the tiniest glimmer of light present because it bothers them, then this demonstrates clearly the power of the subconscious. If you have this type of conditioning, or if you have the opposite problem of needing to keep a light on to get to sleep, and if you have the desire to overcome this, then next time you are in a position where the light (or dark) is bothering you, just relax and repeat to yourself several times something like: "I am not the slightest bit bothered by the light (or the dark), I am now going to fall asleep with ease".

Until fairly recently I had a problem with my eyes, in that, if I ever had to wake up in the middle of the night, say at 3.00 am, I felt intense discomfort in my eyes, to such a degree that I could hardly open them. I always thought that this was a physical problem (even though my eyes were fine during the day!) But then, when I became a father, I started having to wake up regularly at night. Because it was "a problem" that I had to confront, I decided to just take a positive attitude and tell myself: "my eyes are fine" and "I wake up at night with ease". I repeated various suggestions to myself like these many times, and within a short time I actually surprised myself because my eyes ceased to suffer from discomfort if I woke up in the middle of the night - and I wasn't even aware that this condition was caused by my subconscious.

WAKE UP EASILY

Getting up in the morning is a problem for many people. Why is it that some people are able to leap out of bed after a nights sleep feeling totally refreshed and healthy, while others feel half-dead and may take half an hour to just stand up? There could be numerous factors such as excessive consumption of alcohol or drugs, an unhealthy diet, lack of exercise, worry, and so on, but I think that the most important factor is our subconscious programming.

Many people, without realising it, have negative suggestions programmed into their subconscious regarding going to sleep, waking up or getting up, you can use self-suggestion to deal with any of these.

Obviously, if you have trouble getting up on the odd occasion there could be any number of reasons besides the obvious one of getting to bed too late. But for someone who always finds it difficult to wake up or get up, it is useful to look deeper at their subconscious programming and the self-image that this programming has given them. If you have a self-image of having trouble getting up then this will obviously influence how you feel in the morning.

Are any of the following your truths? "I always take at least an hour to get to sleep", I always feel half-dead when I first wake up", "I never feel refreshed after a nights sleep" or "I always have trouble waking up in the morning". If you can relate to any of these, it is important to be aware that they are simply conditioned beliefs which can be changed if you have the desire to change them.

When I was a child, my mother always had an expression that she loved using whenever she was telling me or my sisters to go to bed at night, she would say: "C'mon, up to bed or *you'll never wake up in the morning*!" I must have heard this a few thousand times when I was a child, and considering this, I think that it is no wonder that I often had trouble waking up in the morning! The problem was perpetuated by hearing many comments such as: "He really finds it difficult to wake up" and "it always takes him a while to get up". It is only when I started becoming aware of the power of suggestion, that I was able to transcend this negative conditioning by repeating to myself many times: "I find it really easy to wake up" and "I always wake up easily, feeling totally refreshed, after a wonderful night's sleep."

If you have a problem waking up or getting up, you could try suggestions such as these every night for a few weeks while you are going to sleep and then visualise yourself jumping out of bed, feeling wonderful. Within a very short time your self-image will change to that of a person who sleeps well and gets up really easily. If you can hold this self-image of yourself then this is what will materialise in your life.

Another "truth" that I held until a few years ago is: "I need 8 hours sleep to feel totally refreshed". I believed this because ever since a very young age I heard that the average amount of sleep that everyone requires is 8 hours and so it became my subconscious programming that "I need 8 hours sleep" and I wouldn't feel perfect if I had less. More recently I decided to change my believe to "I only need 6 hours sleep". I did this by using the technique of self-suggestion while visualising myself as a person who only needs 6 hours sleep in order to wake up feeling wonderfully refreshed. Since I started doing this I feel absolutely fine with 6 hours sleep. I only have 7 or 8 hours sleep now if I am feeling very lazy.

It must be remembered that since sleep is an essential activity we mustn't go too far in minimising it. We would be much more in tune with nature if we could forget our watches, ignore the time, and just sleep when tired and get up when refreshed, for many people this isn't a very practical proposition, but it is important to be aware that this is what people did for most of the history of humanity until recently.

WORK EFFORTLESSLY

It is well worth considering the question "what causes tiredness?" Many people would think that the question is hardly worth asking, after all, isn't the answer obviously: "it is just hard work that makes you tired?" However, hard work is only one very small aspect of what can absorb our energy. Within my profession as a teacher I have had days when I have done two hours work and felt exhausted, while there were other days when I could teach 8 hours or more and feel totally fresh and full of energy at the end of the day.

The important thing wasn't how much I was rushing around or how much mental effort I was using to think about the subject, it was more a question of how I was feeling inside while I was teaching. The days that I got more exhausted were times when I felt a little uncomfortable or tense, and the occasions when I felt full of energy at the end of the day were those times when I felt relaxed and was able to give myself to the moment. This observation made me realise that tiredness is caused more by our internal state than by what we are doing.

Tiredness is not caused by what the body does,
it is caused by the state of the body while it does it.

It is true that the state of the body is governed by various physical factors - how efficiently it can eliminate waste and neutralise the toxins produced by metabolic processes, general fitness, dietary factors, and so on. But, apart from these factors, your attitude to your work, determines, to a large extent, the effect that it has on you. If you are able to give yourself to the moment while working, and put yourself into it one hundred percent, you will enjoy it much more and will not get physically drained by the work. Obviously, after a very busy day you could feel healthily tired, but this is a very different feeling, and has a very different effect on your physiology, than to feel drained of energy.

Have you ever experienced sitting in a chair thinking about a job that needs to be done, and while you are just sitting there, you do the job in your mind several times, while thinking something like: "I don't fancy doing that now, I will do it in a minute". Eventually you manage to get yourself out of the chair, do the job, and find that it wasn't all that difficult after all. In this situation you can use more energy just thinking about doing the job than actually doing it.

> *Every time we say: "I must do something"*
> *it takes an incredible amount of energy.*
> *Far more than physically doing it.*
> GITA BELLIN.

Although, from a physicists point of view, forces must be exerted for work to be done, what happens when you think about doing a job is that there are internal changes in your biochemistry which absorb your energy - this will, within a short time, make you feel tired, even if you don't get up from your chair!

Many people give themselves negative suggestions while working which may cause more tiredness than the work itself. They continually tell themselves things like: "This is really tiring", "I can't wait until break-time", "I'm going to be really exhausted this evening", "Isn't this work tedious", and so on. These thoughts can produce internal states that absorb more energy than the job itself. If after doing some work you tell yourself: "I feel absolutely exhausted", then this will have an effect on your body which absorbs even more energy, hence making it come true. However, if you just take a deep breath, hold a good posture and tell yourself "I feel healthy and still have plenty of energy" then this will help your energy to flow and is likely to make you feel much healthier.

There is a way of looking at any task with a happy attitude so that you can enjoy it. If, for example, while washing up you just smile, sing and think pleasant thoughts, then you couldn't possibly feel fed-up and hence the job won't tire you nearly as much as if you were continually focusing on how boring the job is, while feeling resentment for having to engage in such a mundane activity. Singing is known to dissipate many negative emotions and promote good health, especially if the song contains words of joy, optimism or appreciation and has a happy melody. Here are the first few lines of "A spoonful of sugar" from one of the greatest children's films ever made - *Walt Disney's Mary Poppins*:

In every job that must be done there is an element of fun,
you find the fun and..... snap, the jobs a game.
And every task you undertake becomes a piece of cake......
RICHARD M. SHERMAN/ROBERT M. SHERMAN.

ENHANCE YOUR ENERGY

Most people feel a bit lethargic or low in energy at some time or other. There are times when just getting up from the chair or getting out of bed feels like a big effort. What causes this lack of energy? The following list shows ways in which our energy can be lost. Think carefully about which ones might account for your own lack of energy:

- Bad diet.
- Bad posture.
- Lack of exercise.

- Stress/rushing about.
- Destructive pass-times/nervous habits.
- Smoking/drinking alcohol.
- Worry/anger/resentment/hate.
- Cruel or nasty behaviour.
- Self-pity/feeling a victim/feeling helpless.
- Not seeing the beauty around you/not feeling love.
- Being cynical or closed minded.

On a more physical level, the diet is an important factor. If you want to try adjusting your diet for maximum energy, try maximising foods high in *life-energy* (or prana) by eating a primarily vegetarian diet, with as much fresh fruit and vegetables as possible. Minimise your consumption of highly processed foods, tinned products and frozen foods. Also try to avoid the use of the microwave as this absorbs any life-energy that might be present in your foods. As I explained earlier, it is possible that our attitude to what we eat, is more important than what we actually do eat, so, if you do occasionally eat so-called "junk food" don't spend any time worrying about it, just enjoy it. Our level of energy and state of health depends on so many factors, that putting all our attention onto one of them is not always helpful.

The scientific view that our only source of energy is from the food that we eat is grossly oversimplified. Here is a list of things that you can do to boost your energy:

- Self-suggestion - try: "I feel full of life, I am a very energetic person ".
- Visualise yourself in a positive way - hold a self-image of yourself as a loving, healthy, open, energetic person.
- Relax regularly - the more often the better, a few minutes every hour or two sessions of twenty minutes every morning and evening can be very beneficial.

- Don't rush about - give yourself to the moment.
- Avoid any activity which leaves you physically, emotionally or spiritually drained.
- Exercise with awareness - make sure that the exercises you do, leave you feeling healthier than before.
- Smile and laugh frequently.
- Practice conscious breathing - take several deep breaths while imagining the air filling your lungs with energy which travels to every cell of your body.
- Cultivate compassion and kindness.
- Believe in yourself.
- Be mindful of everything you do.
- See the beauty in people and be open with them.
- Love and appreciate everyone and everything in your life.
- Go for regular walks while thinking positively.
- Visit parks and other natural places regularly.
- Look at a plant or insect close up and observe its natural beauty.

The last few of these draw attention to the important point that our level of energy is not only determined by how fit we are but also by our level of contact with nature. If we could be totally in harmony with ourselves and with life, then it might be possible that we would never get tired since we would be connected to the ultimate source of energy - the universe itself.

There are many positive benefits of short, but frequent, relaxation sessions, but one of the main ones is to help you learn to pay greater attention to your body's signals - as you sit quietly become aware of any tensions, uneasy feelings, or inner discomfort that your body may be conveying to you for good reason. If you then make appropriate modifications in your behaviour, responding to your body with love and care you will notice an immediate enhancement in your level of health.

ENERGY ENHANCING VISUALISATION:
The following is a very simple, yet effective, visualisation exercise to enhance your energy. It is a wonderful exercise to do when you are feeling low in energy, and it is such a simple exercise that you could do it at any odd moment whenever it feels convenient.

Visit a park, your back garden, or any place of natural beauty, take a few deep breaths while observing the beauty of everything around you. Imagine an invisible energy connecting you to the trees, flowers and grass. Now, as you breathe, feel this energy flowing into you, through your lungs, and energising every cell of your body. Appreciate the immense beauty around you and feel yourself connecting with it, as you breathe you will become more energised. This could take up only a minute of your time, but if you were to do it every day, you would notice a considerable change in your level of energy and your feeling of inner peace.

A final word

You must now be aware not only of the immense power that you have within you to achieve great heights, but also of the fact that you can "will" yourself to happiness or misery, to success or failure, to health or sickness.

Obviously the quality of your life depends to a certain extent on external circumstances, but it depends to a greater extent on what is within you, on your attitude, your thoughts, your imagination and your subconscious programming. You have control over all of these things - if you believe that you have!

The key to achieving, is to have dreams, but don't live for the dreams, live for the moment, here and now. To make dreams become reality you need to form a goal, get clear in your mind what you desire, verbalise and visualise the desired outcome, believe that it is achievable, let go of self-limiting beliefs and trust in your abilities to achieve whatever your heart desires. Also, trust that life is on your side and develop an appreciation for whatever life offers you.

May you now be free from the bondage of fear and self-imposed limitations, and trust in yourself to deal with any experience and create the fantastic situations that you desire. I wish you a wonderful life.

Bibliography

Ageless body, timeless mind - Deepak Chopra. Published by Rider 1993.

The power of positive thinking - Norman Vincent Peale. Published by Cedar books.

Handbook to higher consciousness - Ken Keyes Jr. Published by Loveline books.

The Dynamic Laws of Healing - Catherine Ponder. Published by Devorss & Co.

Feel the fear and do it anyway - Susan Jeffers. Published by Arrow Books Limited.

Thorsons introductory guide to Hypnotherapy - Hellmut W. A. Karle. Published by Thorsons 1992.

Living in the Light - Shakti Gawain. Published by Eden Grove Editions.

Staying on the path - Dr. Wayne W. Dyer. Published by Hay House, Inc.

The Celestine Prophecy, An adventure - James Redfield. Published by Bantam books.

The Celestine Prophecy, An experiential guide - James Redfield and Carol Adrienne. Published by Bantam books.

You can have it all - Arnold Patent. Published by Money Mastery Publishing, 1984.

A guide for the advanced soul - Susan Hayward. Published by In-tune books.

The nature of personal reality - Jane Roberts. Published by Prentice Hall, Inc.

Improve your vision without glasses or contact lenses - the American Vision Institute. Published by fireside books.

Better Sight Without Glasses - Harry Benjamin. Published by Thorsons.

About the author

Tycho graduated from university in 1982 with a B.Sc. degree in Physics and Astrophysics. He then went on to become a professional musician and teacher of Guitar, Piano and Bass. In 1988 he obtained an Open University degree in mathematics and science and is currently a part-time lecturer in Mathematics and Physics. The rest of his time is divided between his writing and the running of *The British Centre for Stress Management*, which he founded in 1997.

After finishing his first degree in 1982 he set off around Europe on a personal pilgrimage that was to become the inspirational springboard for this series of books. During his time abroad, and since, he has extensively studied eastern philosophy including Yoga, Buddhism, and Martial arts comparing the principles of Eastern and Western religions and the various interpretations of the concept of God. His disattachment to any religion or doctrine has given him the scope to freely move among the various teachings with an open but necessarily doubting mind.

His path has led him to seek the universal roots of spirituality, extracting the essence of the many aspects of philosophical teachings and religions, in the firm knowledge that each has its own treasures to uncover. His discoveries have led him primarily to acknowledge the relationships between the spirit, the mind, and the body working together in order to reach the highest quality of life.

Tycho's background was based on good conventional family values with encouragement towards individual self-discovery. These foundations created in the author a dual loyalty - a respect for established beliefs, both past and present, and an adventurous spirit, exploring new territory, questioning and probing the fertile terrain of life's secret gardens.

This book is both comprehensive and inspiring, and the reader will doubtless find themselves irresistibly launching out on their own voyage of discovery.

Andrea Photiou.

Tycho is the founder and director of *The British Centre for Stress Management* situated in Enfield, (North London). The centre offers various courses and workshops designed for your personal growth and spiritual development. For more information, either phone or send a stamped addressed envelope to the address below:

The British Centre for Stress Management
228 Baker Street,
Enfield EN1 3JY
Middlesex.

Tel (0181) 350 9600

Tycho is also the Founder and Director of *The National Society for Personal Growth.* This society exists primarily to link together like-minded people, for interesting meetings, discussions, and exchange of information about topics of mutual interest.

Some of the topics of interest include:
♦ Self-confidence and self-esteem.
♦ What is meditation?
♦ Finding inner peace.
♦ Realising your full potential.
♦ Goal setting.
♦ Self-empowerment and responsibility.
♦ The technique of self-suggestion.
♦ Trusting in life - learning to take risks.
♦ Overcoming the fear of death.
♦ Enhancing your immunity.
♦ The power of the mind.
♦ Holistic medicine.
♦ The unity of all things.
♦ Tapping into inner wisdom.
♦ Learning from every experience.
♦ Health Topics.
♦ Hypnosis.
♦ Homeopathy.

Membership to the Society costs only £12 for 1 year. For this small fee, you will receive:

☞ A free 120 page book of inspirational quotations.

☞ Bi-monthly articles written by Tycho or Andrea.

☞ The opportunity to meet up with other local members.

☞ Information about courses and workshops offered at *The British Centre for Stress Management.*

☞ Gatherings of society members with the intention of meeting like-minded people and discussing topics of mutual interest.

☞ Occasional book reviews and the facility to exchange books with other society members.

We will circulate a list of members once or twice a year as required.

To become a society member or for more information phone (0181) 350 9600. Alternatively write to 228 Bakers street, Enfield, EN1 3 JY.

Address has changed
Please phone 020 8350 9600